Rustic Joyful Food

Meant to Share

Rustic *Joyful* Food

Meant to Share

DANIELLE KARTES

Photography by Michael Kartes

Copyright © 2020 by Danielle Kartes
Cover and internal design © 2020 by Sourcebooks
Cover design by Brittany Vibbert/Sourcebooks
Cover and internal images © Michael Kartes
Internal design by Jillian Rahn

Sourcebooks and the colophon are registered trademarks of Sourcebooks.

All rights reserved. No part of this book may be reproduced in any form or by any electronic or mechanical means including information storage and retrieval systems—except in the case of brief quotations embodied in critical articles or reviews—without permission in writing from its publisher, Sourcebooks.

This publication is designed to provide accurate and authoritative information in regard to the subject matter covered. It is sold with the understanding that the publisher is not engaged in rendering legal, accounting, or other professional service. If legal advice or other expert assistance is required, the services of a competent professional person should be sought.—*From a Declaration of Principles Jointly Adopted by a Committee of the American Bar Association and a Committee of Publishers and Associations*

All brand names and product names used in this book are trademarks, registered trademarks, or trade names of their respective holders. Sourcebooks is not associated with any product or vendor in this book.

Published by Sourcebooks
P.O. Box 4410, Naperville, Illinois 60567-4410
(630) 961-3900
sourcebooks.com

Library of Congress Cataloging-in-Publication Data is on file with the publisher.

Printed and bound in China.
OGP 10 9 8 7 6 5 4 3 2

This book is dedicated to my dad,

Sergeant Major Michael Hawkins,

who taught me to work hard and give grace.

Contents

◆◇◆

Introduction   xvii

For Friendship + Company   1

Creamy Tomato Baked Ziti with Garlic Toast and Salami
    Chopped Salad   7
Cassoulet with Chicken Thighs and Sausages and Smashed
    Cucumber and Pesto Salad   9
Coq au Vin with Pancetta Polenta and Sautéed Swiss Chard   13
Beer-Braised Chuck Roast with Red Onions, Parsnips,
    and Carrots; Glazed Carrots and Parsnips; and Sour
    Cream Smashed Potatoes   15
Cheddar and Dill Baked Potato Soup   19
Bacon, Tomato, and Mushroom Campanelle with Spinach
    and Parmesan Salad   20
Sausage and Leek Puff Pastry Pie with Baby Greens and Red
    Pesto Dressing   22
Tuscan Veggie and Chickpea Stew and Cheesy Scallion
    Soda Bread   24
Ground Beef Stroganoff with Parmesan Skillet Broccoli   27

Steak "Dianna" with Creamy Cauliflower Mashed Potatoes and
  Stovetop Ratatouille   28
Pistachio-Crusted Chicken Cutlets with Simple Heirloom Tomato
  and Ricotta Salad   31

For Comfort + Family   35

Creamy Sausage and Mushroom Lasagna and Boston
  Buttermilk Salad   39
Lydia's Casserole (Creamy Celery, Leek, Potato, and Kielbasa
  Sausage Bake) with Mixed Greens and Lemony Honey Mustard   41
Chimichurri Chicken Meatballs with Herbed Greek Yogurt,
  Red Quinoa, and Green Beans   45
Baked Salmon with Strawberry Basil Relish and Herb and
  Parmesan Israeli Couscous   48
Quick Creole Shrimp Étouffée with Butter Lettuce and Mushroom
  Salad   51
Enchilada Meatballs (Albondigas) with Spanish Rice and
  Refried Beans   53
Sweet 'n' Sour Chicken with Cheap Chow Mein   57
Pesto and Mozzarella Pasta with Italian Rocket and
  Chicken Salad   59
Boneless Braised Pork Spareribs with Garlicky Chanterelles
  and Spaetzle   63
Shrimp and Chive Penne and Garlic Knots   64
Eggplant Parmesan, Frisée Salad, and Cheesy Breadsticks   66

For Fun + Littles   69

Sticky, Spicy Oven-Baked Baby Back Ribs with Sesame Broccoli
  and Rice   73
Grilled Lamb Kabobs and Red Quinoa and Tomato Grain Salad   74

Sheet Pan Chicken Nachos, Fresh Guacamole, and Chili-Lime
 Pineapple Spears 77
Classic Baked Shells and Cheese with Oven-Roasted
 Lemon-Pepper Asparagus 79
Garlic and Anchovy Spaghetti with Bread Crumbs and Apple
 Cider Brussels Sprouts 80
The Last Meatball Recipe You'll Ever Need, Creamy Orzo,
 and Spinach and Basil Pesto 83
Ranch Smash Burgers, Garlicky Green Beans, and Potato
 Wedges with Sour Cream Dressing 85
Buttermilk Grilled Chicken, Parmesan Ditalini and Peas, and
 Buttery Dinner Rolls 88
Barbecue Chicken Legs, Zucchini and Fresh Corn Fritters with
 Sun-Dried Tomato Aioli, and Creamy Traditional Coleslaw 91
Focaccia MLTs (Mozzarella, Lettuce, and Tomato) with Sweet
 Potato Fries 93
Creamy Tomato and Pumpkin Soup and Pan-Fried Cheese
 Sandwiches 97

For Love 99

Crispy Sweet Chili and Sesame Shrimp with Ginger
 Peanut Noodles 105
Fiery, Sweet Asian Salmon with Rice Noodles and Quick
 Pickled Cucumbers 107
Garlic and Lemon Cacio e Pepe with Roasted Artichokes and Aioli 110
Pan-Seared Dill and Caper Halibut, Black Pepper and Parmesan
 Risotto, and Garlicky Asparagus 113
Lobster Dinner Splurge, Dreamy Dauphinoise Potatoes, and
 Mâché Caesar Salad 115
Zesty Buffalo-Style Rack of Lamb with Crunchy Celery and
 Blue Cheese Salad 118

Spicy, Fresh Heirloom Tomato Bucatini with Brie and
    Heirloom Tomato Toast   121
Melon with Basil and Prosciutto, Peach and Heirloom Tomato
    Panzanella, and Charcuterie and Cheese   122
Lovely Toast x 3: Fresh Fig and Soft Cheese, Soft-Boiled
    Eggs and Green Beans with Hazelnut and Lemon Vinaigrette,
    and Chicken Caesar   127

Sweets 131

Apple Cinnamon Monkey Bread	135
Cherry Pie Bars	136
Flaky Cream Biscuits	139
Lime Tres Leches Cake	141
Pumpkin Tiramisu	143
Tender Gingerbread Cake	144
Vanilla Panna Cotta with Citrus Caramel	147
Short-Crust Sour Cherry Cobbler	148
Double Peanut Marshmallow Treats	150
Apricot and Chocolate Rolls	151
Chocolate Chip Pumpkin Bread	152
Pineapple Cloud Cake	155
Cream Coconut Cake	156
Creamy Lime Tart	159
Basic Not-Basic Chocolate Cream Pie	161
Magic Shell and Pistachio Sundaes	162
Chocolate Peanut Butter Tart	165
Chocolate Almond Coconut Granola Sundae	166
Wild Dried Blueberry Pound Cake	167
Churros con Chocolate	168

Olive Oil and Espresso Dark Chocolate Cake with Cream
    Cheese Buttercream and Caramel   171
Apple Cranberry Shortbread Crumble   172

Noah's Apple Cake	175
One-Pan Lava Cake	175
Molten Chocolate and Caramel Cakes	176
Apple Butter Crumb Cake	179
Caramelized Banana Cream Pudding	180

Drinks 183

Homemade Limoncello	187
Crème de Cassis	189
Irish Cream Mason Jars to Go	193
Mom's Wine Punch	194
Pear Brandy	195
Beer and Grapefruit Spritzers	197
Homemade Cold Brew with Brown Sugar Syrup	198
Virgin Mary Mix	201
Cinnamon Hot Chocolate with Soft Whipped Cream	202
Homemade Chai Tea Concentrate	203
Mulled Wine	205
Hot Lemonade Tea	206
Strawberry Bellini	209
Creamy Coconut and Vodka Punch	210
Peachy Basil Lemonade	213

Closing Thoughts 215

Index 221

About the Author 233

The RUSTIC *Joyful* FOOD MANIFESTO

At Rustic Joyful Food, we believe that life is good *right now*, no matter what.
Life isn't good only when you have it all together, with the perfect job and enough money in the bank, or only when you have the most beautiful kitchen and a refrigerator loaded with the finest ingredients. There is happiness in the middle. Be grateful; gratitude and joy go hand in hand. Every moment is an opportunity to choose joy, even when life is hard. *You are going to be okay*; you were made to weather difficult things. Use what you have available to you in the kitchen and in life, and then, with a smile, start cooking.

Introduction

Life is good right now, *in the moment.*

You don't have to lead a life of extravagance, have the best of everything, matching china, or a big, beautiful room for entertaining...to share. Money may be tight, the struggle very real, and yet we can still find ways to love the people in our lives through simply feeding them. I've always said that to feed someone is to truly love them.

There have been times in my life when it felt like the cupboard contained just enough to feed my own family, but somehow, if someone I knew needed a meal because they were sick or they merely wanted some company, we found a way to make it work. All the dried pasta odds and ends happen to make an incredible bake once all the wildly different shapes are boiled and tossed with sauce; just a bit more broth or water makes another serving of gravy or stew in the end. Just deciding we are gonna make it work, almost as if through sheer will, somehow seems to double the portions in the pot. There is nourishment, too, in the stretching. As humans, as beings capable of empathy, sharing is in our bones.

Rustic Joyful Food, at its core, revolves around the idea that life is good right now, *in the moment*. In spite of life's difficulties and even though we might not have it all figured out, we have the capacity to find joy. Cooking and feeding people is about loving the journey, not having it all put together. It's about laughter and making memories, not matching dishes or grand houses (although, it must be said, those things are lovely too). Having friends over for dinner on a weeknight is not about impressing them. It's about good food that nourishes the soul and giving people a sense of welcome. It's about providing a pit stop during the week, a recharge, enjoying a big pot of soup with a hunk of bread and butter. It's a respite from life. And it's about enjoying all these things in the moment, even if the rest of your life is decidedly imperfect.

We are meant for community, and our hearts long for fellowship and laughter. We are designed for joy, specifically the kind that arises from time well spent with others. Sometimes we want to wait until things feel perfect. We will have people over when we know them better, or we will give when we have more to spare. I know that God loves openhandedness. He is generous and loves it when His children are generous. Because it is easy to find ourselves living inwardly, focusing on work, the kids, the minutiae of life, etc., it's imperative that we occasionally pause to acknowledge our built-in desire to reach out in the spirit of community.

At this time in my life, I felt as though I was barely making it through.

Several years ago, we lived in a small condo. During this time, my husband, Michael, and I were new parents, our restaurant Minoela had closed six months prior, and we decided to produce a cookbook to preserve the recipes we had so enjoyed preparing for customers. At this time in my life, I felt as though I was barely making it through. I wasn't very adept at getting to know my neighbors, and I didn't ever feel like saying hello. I'd scurry into my house from my car, often not bringing my head up, just grabbing Noah from his car seat and hustling on our way.

One day around this time, my good friend Jeff and I happened to be outside near my front door, shooting a dish of short ribs and browned butter carrots for my first book. Jeff was a photographer. Short ribs were wildly expensive, and the plan, as was often the case, was to photograph the dish and eat it for dinner that night. As we were wrapping the shoot, my neighbors pulled into their parking spot beside mine. My neighbors were a middle-aged couple I had often seen around the complex, though I didn't know their names. The woman hopped out of the driver's seat and hurried around to the passenger's side, opening the door. Her partner was usually the picture of health, rather handsome, but now, as he stepped out, he appeared frail and sickly. It occurred to me that I hadn't seen him around the complex as of late. She held his arm as he walked slowly down the sidewalk, past my door, and they paused at my porch. Admittedly, it probably looks pretty funny to see dishes set and arranged just so on a concrete porch with reflectors looming over them if you've never seen it before. Tom said it looked and smelled delicious. We laughed and visited for just a moment about what we were doing, then they went home, Jeff left, and I took the food inside.

I stood in silence for a moment, thinking. I put a piece of foil over the short ribs and carrots, put the creamy mashed potatoes into a container, and carried the food the short distance to Tom and Mary's front door. It was a feast, the kind of food that your mama makes you—real food. Food to heal the heart. Comfort food. And they were delighted. Tom sat bundled in blankets on their couch, and Mary's eyes were dancing.

"Really? You're giving us this food?"

"Yes!" I said. "Please enjoy." I didn't know what illness Tom was suffering from, but I knew he appreciated the lightness of that moment.

Several weeks passed, then one morning, there was a knock at my door. It was Mary. She had my serving dish hugged tightly across her chest. Before she spoke, I knew. Her eyes welled with tears, and with a big smile, she said, "Tom passed away."

I reached out to hug her, and there we stood, strangers but familiar, connected by a meal and an open heart. We cried together. She said, "That food you gave us was the most delicious we'd ever had. It was the last meal Tom ate. He loved every bite. Thank you." She handed me my dish, and we said goodbye. I'll never forget her. I'll never forget Tom.

We *need* to be fed and loved as a community, as a society, as a people. Food is the great equalizer. We all must eat, and we all must move past whatever insecurities we carry as individuals and share a good meal. This book is filled with recipes that aim to serve just that purpose, complete suppers meant to nourish, to drive laughter, and to heal. It's food to be shared in your home, with those you love. It's food that's easily packed up for a neighbor, friend, or family member in need of being heard and feeling loved. No matter what, do not grow weary in doing good. Don't question whether or not to give—just give and follow your heart. A container of homemade soup etches a memory into someone's soul and serves as a reminder that they are not forgotten—they are loved.

For Friendship + Company

hos·pi·tal·i·ty
/ˌhäspəˈtalədē/

hospitable treatment, reception, or disposition <thanked our hosts for their hospitality>
Synonyms: friendliness, hospitableness, welcome, warm reception, helpfulness, neighborliness, warmth,
warmheartedness, kindness, kindheartedness, congeniality, geniality, sociability, conviviality, cordiality,
amicability, amenability, generosity, liberality, bountifulness, openhandedness.
—Merriam-Webster Collegiate Dictionary

Have you ever been invited into someone's home and immediately felt at ease? As if the table was set specifically for you? As if things on shelves were so beautifully arranged that it was just for you? There are several women in my life who really embody this level of personalized hospitality, and it does not go unappreciated.

Specifically, I had a friend for many years who was the epitome of elegant. She was roughly ten years my senior and effortless in all she did. She introduced me to Lillet and lavender sugar and French linens. Her style was so chic, yet being in her home made you feel good about who you were. She would always set out small trays of snacks on lovely antique serve ware, which was an incredible revelation for me; I didn't think you could do that! I don't think I ever visited her home without leaving with armfuls of beautiful things, from antiques to fresh grown produce to stunning pastel fresh eggs from the chickens she kept. If you marveled at just about anything in her home, she'd give it to you, no questions asked. She'd simply pack it up in linens, place it in a vintage market basket, and send you home with it. It was remarkable. She never seemed to have too much, just the right amount of special things, and none of it was so precious that she wouldn't part with it if she thought gifting it would brighten your day. She was the queen of thoughtfulness and grace. The way she prized her loved ones

I can't help but get overwhelmed with excitement at making my home a place where friends feel loved.

was special. She introduced me to so many women who loved in that very same way, all of whom would gather together often for the kind of dinner parties I thought you only read about in books. I learned how to welcome other people into my home from her. I learned how to love them well from a true hospitality perspective. I treasured every moment spent in her home learning from her.

She was once a photographer and had the loveliest of curated items used for shooting food scenes. One day, she called me and said, "You know, I've been going through some things, and I just think you might give them a good home. They're things I'll never need or use again and much of it's from France. Would you like to come pick up a few things?" I couldn't have prepared myself for the beauty within the old letter courier basket she presented. When I arrived at her house, it was there on her table, perfectly packaged, just waiting for me. There were French yogurt containers and silver plate flatware, old cooling racks, and jam jars circa the 1940s. The textured linens were absolutely the very best linens I'd ever seen. This basket was chock-full of things I never could have purchased on my own. I've never been to the *brocantes* in France, where she brought many of these possessions home from. This was a few years ago now, and these treasures remain some of my most cherished belongings. They've appeared in dozens of my own food photos, and they most certainly grace the pages of this book. For me, these items represent friendship. I know we aren't supposed to love *stuff*, but when the stuff helps communicate a vision I have for presenting food, which ultimately serves others, I can't help but get overwhelmed with excitement at making my home a place where friends feel loved.

I've always loved opening my home but never knew the value of doing it beautifully—not in a way that's ostentatious or shows off but, for instance, by simply removing snacks from their boxes and placing them into homemade ceramic bowls. The snacks are suddenly elevated, beautiful. I am an avid thrift-store shopper. I find delight in secondhand, well-worn items. I don't spend grand amounts of money, and I don't have serve ware or china I don't use because they might be too valuable. The value is in using them. Snipping branches from my yard and placing them into old jars or thrifted vases can look exquisite, lived-in, and inviting. Fresh

hand towels in the bathroom or fresh fruit already out and ready when guests arrive can make all the difference. Recently, a friend told me how much they enjoyed that whenever they visited, we had soft, pleasant music playing quietly. Now, when I have people over, I think of ways I can bless them beyond dinner alone. I've always grown fresh tomatoes and herbs, not only to enjoy with my family but also to give away to treasured visitors. These little things can truly reveal for your guest the heart you have for making them comfortable.

Each time I visit someone's home and sit at their table or on their couch, I delight in getting to see just a small slice of their day-to-day life. When I go to my sister's house, I flop onto her couch, and she calls from the kitchen what she has to offer in the way of drinks, and then she'll join me with a cup of whatever and just visit while our kiddos play. This sort of time is restorative. My sister introduced me to cold brew coffee, and since then, I think I've sent cold brew and brown sugar syrup home with a dozen friends who've stopped by to visit and unload life's burdens while our kids play. It's the kind of sharing I love best, deeper because it works on two levels. There's shared conversation, laughter, maybe even tears, and afterward a gift to take home, something tangible to mark the occasion.

I used to feel like everything had to be utterly perfect—scrubbed floors, zero clutter, all dishes in cupboards, none in the sink—to invite someone over. But now I know that what I have to offer in the way of my home and space is ultimately just an extension of me, and I really like me. I've always liked me and who God created me to be—sometimes messy and a bit scattered, busy with the activity of everyday living. I think when we act from a place of self-love, it is so much easier to love others. I want people to feel good about who they are and just a tiny bit special inside my house, utterly clean and clutter-free or not. Friendships thrive with a little grace, and the more we allow people, the more apt they will be to return it in kind.

These meals were designed with friendship and comfort in mind. When your favorite people drop in, these dishes will feed one part of you as the conversation and connection feed another. Be brave enough to give friends a place to be themselves, with no expectations or requirements. They might need the kind of healing only your hospitality can provide. You just might need a little of what they have to offer too. In every case, these meals will help salve the wounds or accentuate the joy of living.

Creamy Tomato Baked Ziti with Garlic Toast and Salami Chopped Salad

Prep time: 15 minutes • Bake time: 30 minutes • Yield: 6 servings

1 (16-ounce) box ziti

¼ cup butter

2 tablespoons olive oil

½ cup finely diced onion

1 pinch crushed red pepper flakes

Salt and pepper to taste

3 cloves fresh garlic, chopped

¼ cup all-purpose flour

4 cups milk

1 (15-ounce) can diced tomatoes
  in juice or sauce

1 tablespoon tomato paste

1½ cups shredded w cheese

1½ cup shredded mozzarella
  cheese

PAIR WITH:

- *Peachy Basil Lemonade (page 213)*
- *Chocolate Peanut Butter Tart (page 165)*
- *Lime Tres Leches Cake (page 141)*

Preheat oven to 350° and butter a 9-by-13-inch pan. Cook the pasta according to the package instructions for al dente results. While pasta is cooking, prepare the sauce. In a large pot, melt the butter over medium heat and add the olive oil, onion, pepper flakes, and salt and pepper. Once the onion is soft, roughly 3 to 4 minutes, add the garlic and cook an additional minute. Add the flour and cook 3 to 4 minutes. Add the milk, tomatoes, and tomato paste. Stir until the mixture begins to thicken. Add half the cheeses, then taste for seasoning. You will need a bit more salt than you may be used to in order to season the pasta. Combine sauce with noodles and pour into the buttered 9-by-13-inch pan. Cover with remaining cheese and bake 20 minutes until cheese is melted.

Garlic Toast

Bake time: 15 minutes • Yield: 6 servings

1 (roughly) 15-ounce artisan
  bread loaf

1 cup shredded parmesan cheese

½ cup butter, melted

½ cup finely chopped parsley

2 cloves fresh garlic, smashed
  and chopped

2 tablespoons olive oil

Salt and pepper to taste

Slice the bread into 12 even slices. Combine all the other ingredients in a bowl. Spoon one tablespoon of the garlic-butter mixture onto one side of each slice of bread, then assemble the sliced bread back into a loaf and wrap tightly in foil. Bake 15 minutes. Make sure the seam is facing up when baking so butter does not leak out.

Recipe continues on next page

» *Continued*

Salami Chopped Salad

Prep time: 10 minutes • Yield: 4–6 servings

SALAD

4 cups chopped romaine lettuce

4 cups chopped cabbage

6 hard boiled eggs, quartered

1 pound salami, sliced into strips

1½ cups cured black olives
  (canned work great)

1½ cups cherry tomatoes

1 bunch scallions, chopped

1 cucumber, sliced

½ cup thinly sliced red onion

DRESSING

½ cup olive oil

¼ cup balsamic vinegar

1 teaspoon Dijon mustard

1 teaspoon dried oregano

½ teaspoon crushed red pepper
  flakes

Juice of 1 lemon

Salt and pepper to taste

Layer the salad ingredients in a large mixing bowl in the order they appear. Mix gently to evenly distribute the ingredients. Whisk together the dressing ingredients in a separate bowl. Spoon the dressing over individual portions of the salad, not the entire bowl.

Cassoulet with Chicken Thighs and Sausages and Smashed Cucumber and Pesto Salad

When researching recipes for this classic French stew, I found them to be complicated, some requiring two to three days of prep. I couldn't help but think there must be a better way. Then, as I got into the ingredients lists, it was mainly duck and stuffed sausages. I'll let you in on a teeny tiny secret: chicken thighs, braised low and slow, will win a taste battle with duck confit any day. Shh, don't go spreading that secret around anywhere. But take a look at how we turned a three-day cooking marathon into a two-hour Sunday braise.

Cassoulet with Chicken Thighs and Sausages

Prep time: 30 minutes • Inactive cook time: 90 minutes • Yield: 4–6 servings

1½ pounds sausage in casings (we chose Linguica sausage)*

2 tablespoons olive oil

6 boneless, skinless chicken thighs

3–4 slices pancetta or prosciutto or unsmoked bacon; lightly smoked bacon works fine as well

2 medium shallots, chopped

1 medium carrot, diced

1 teaspoon *piment d'Espelette***

1 teaspoon onion powder

1 pinch crushed red pepper flakes

2 sprigs rosemary

3 cloves fresh garlic, chopped

1 (28-ounce) can whole peeled tomatoes in juice

2 (15-ounce) cans white cannellini beans, drained and rinsed

Salt and pepper to taste

> **PAIR WITH:**
> - *Mulled Wine, served chilled (page 205)*
> - *Caramelized Banana Cream Pudding (page 180)*

* *Mild Italian sausage or bratwurst work beautifully in this dish. Use at least one sausage per person eating the meal. I chose Linguica for its spicy, aromatic flavor and its deep reddish color.*

** *Piment d'Espelette is a powdered, mild, French pepper, similar to paprika. If you can't find piment d'Espelette, paprika works just fine.*

Preheat the oven to 350°. Brown the sausages in the olive oil in an enamel-covered Dutch oven or cast iron pan with a lid over medium heat, 3 to 4 minutes. Cook them just enough to get color, not all the way through. Remove and set aside. Season the chicken thighs lightly with salt and pepper, and brown them on either side without cooking through, then remove. Fond—the caramelized bits of goodness—will begin building on the bottom of the pan. Add the bacon, shallots, and carrots. Caramelize the bacon. Season with *piment d'Espelette*, salt and pepper, onion

Recipe continues on next page

Continued

powder, and pepper flakes. Add the rosemary sprigs. Once the bacon is caramelized and the shallots are cooked, add the garlic. Add a touch more olive oil if the pan needs it. Cook the garlic for about a minute, then add the tomatoes. Work the brown caramelized bits from the bottom of the pan with a wooden spoon. This process is called *deglazing*. Bring the tomatoes to a simmer, and add the beans. Tuck the browned chicken and sausages into the stew. Bake covered for 60 to 90 minutes. Once the stew is finished baking, top with crunchy pan-fried bread crumbs and enjoy.

Pan-Fried Butter and Herb Bread Crumbs

Cook Time: 10 minutes • Yield: 4–6 servings

1 cube butter

3 cups stale Italian country bread, torn into bite-sized pieces

½ cup chopped parsley

1 teaspoon chopped fresh rosemary

Salt and pepper to taste

Melt the butter in a large skillet, and add the bread, herbs, salt, and pepper. Sauté until the bread begins to brown. Serve warm on top of the cassoulet.

Smashed Cucumber and Pesto Salad

Prep time: 5 minutes • Serving: just over 1 cup

SPINACH AND BASIL PESTO (NUT FREE)

3 cups baby spinach

1 cup fresh sweet basil leaves

¾ cup olive oil

½ cup grated parmesan cheese

1 clove fresh garlic

Juice and zest of 1 lemon

Salt and pepper to taste

SMASHED CUCUMBER SALAD

1 English cucumber

2 cups baby spinach

1 cup cherry tomatoes, halved

½ cup fresh miniature mozzarella balls (*ciliegine*)

½ cup prepared spinach and basil pesto

Whirl all the pesto ingredients in a food processor. Using the pulse option yields a pesto that retains some texture and won't be overly smooth. Refrigerate and use within 3 days.

To complete the salad, break the cucumber into three sections, then break those sections in half lengthwise and slice into bite-sized pieces. Combine the cucumber, spinach, tomatoes, and mozzarella in a mixing bowl, and mix with the pesto.

Coq au Vin with Pancetta Polenta and Sautéed Swiss Chard

Coq au Vin

Prep Time: 20 minutes • Cook Time: 20 minutes • Yield: 4 servings

6–8 bone-in, skin-on chicken thighs

2 tablespoons olive oil

4 carrots, peeled and sliced on the bias

3 sprigs lemon thyme

1 fresh bay leaf, dry is fine

1 cup frozen pearl onions

½ red onion, sliced

2 cups cremini or baby bella brown mushrooms, halved

4–6 cloves fresh garlic, smashed

2 cups light red wine, like a pinot noir

Salt and pepper to taste

> **PAIR WITH:**
>
> • *Creamy Lime Tart (page 159)*
>
> • *Apple Cranberry Shortbread Crumble (page 172)*

Preheat your oven to 350°. Season both sides of the chicken thighs with salt and pepper. Brown the chicken thighs in a heavy-bottomed cast iron pan (preferably enamel covered, but any pan that can go from stove-top browning to oven braising is okay) in the olive oil, skin side down, until golden and crisp, about 4 to 5 minutes. Remove the chicken from the pan and set aside. Sauté the vegetables and herbs for 2 to 3 minutes in the chicken drippings and then add the garlic. Nestle the chicken thighs among the veggies, skin side up, and add the wine. Add 1 cup water and season the entire thing again with salt and pepper. Cover tightly with a lid or foil and bake for 60 to 90 minutes or until the chicken is fall-apart tender and the sauce has reduced. Serve atop pancetta polenta with a side of lightly dressed greens.

Pancetta Polenta

Prep time: 5 minutes • Cook time: 20–25 minutes • Yield: 4–6 servings

1 cup pancetta or uncured bacon, chopped

½ cup finely chopped onion

1 tablespoon olive oil

1 clove fresh garlic, smashed

4–5 cups chicken stock

1 cup dry polenta (I prefer Bob's Red Mill Polenta Corn Grits because of its quick cooking time)

Salt and pepper to taste

1 cup heavy cream

1 cup grated parmesan cheese

Brown the pancetta or bacon and onion in the olive oil in a large saucepan over medium heat. Add the garlic and stir for roughly 1 minute. Add the stock, polenta, and salt and pepper. Cook

Recipe continues on next page

» Continued

10 to 15 minutes, stirring constantly. This cooking process can take 15 to 40 minutes depending on the type of polenta, cornmeal, or grits being used. Once polenta is fully cooked and tender and has absorbed the liquid, remove from heat and add the heavy cream and parmesan cheese. The polenta should be smooth and flavorful, with good texture but no hard bite when chewing. Season with salt and pepper.

Sautéed Swiss Chard

Prep time: 5 minutes • Cook time: 15 minutes • Yield: 4–6 servings

1 bunch red swiss chard, roughly 4–5 cups chopped

2 tablespoons olive oil

2 cloves fresh garlic, chopped

Salt and pepper to taste

Sauté the swiss chard in oil and 2 tablespoons water over medium heat in a large nonstick skillet until water has evaporated. Add the chopped garlic, and season with salt and pepper. Sauté 2 to 3 minutes more and serve. The leaves should be very wilted, almost caramelized. The stems should be crisp tender.

Beer-Braised Chuck Roast with Red Onions, Parsnips, and Carrots; Glazed Carrots and Parsnips; and Sour Cream Smashed Potatoes

Chuck Roast

Prep time: 10 minutes • Braising time: 5 hours • Yield: 4–6 people

2 tablespoons butter

2 large red onions, sliced in thick, one-inch slices

1 3-pound chuck roast, nicely marbled with fat

Salt and pepper to taste (for most meats, 1 teaspoon salt per pound works nicely)

1 (12-ounce) medium-bodied beer, such as a pilsner or golden ale, not IPA

> **PAIR WITH:**
>
> • *Virgin Mary Mix (page 201)*
>
> • *Molten Chocolate and Caramel Cakes (page 176)*
>
> • *Basic Not-Basic Chocolate Cream Pie (page 161)*

Preheat oven to 300°. Place the butter and onions in a large oven-safe pot with a tight-fitting lid. Sauté over medium heat for 2 to 3 minutes, then place the roast on top of the onions. Season liberally with salt and pepper. Pour the beer into the pot, keeping the pour away from the meat so as not to disturb the salt and pepper. Cover the pot with the lid, and place in the oven for 5 hours. Check the meat periodically to make sure the liquid hasn't completely evaporated. You should be left with at least 2 cups of liquid once the braising is finished.

Glazed Carrots and Parsnips

Prep time: 5 minutes • Cook time: 10–15 minutes • Yield: 4–6 servings

5 medium carrots, peeled

3 medium parsnips, peeled

1 tablespoon butter

¼–½ cup braising liquid from the roast (whatever you can spare, leaving some for final plating)

2 cloves fresh garlic, smashed and chopped

2 teaspoons brown sugar

2 teaspoons Dijon mustard

Salt and pepper to taste

Slice the carrots and parsnips in half lengthwise, then into thirds. Heat the butter in a large skillet. Add the sliced parsnips and carrots. Sauté 2 to 3 minutes. Add the braising liquid, garlic, sugar, and mustard. Continue cooking until vegetables are tender and liquid has reduced by half. Season with salt and pepper to taste.

Recipe continues on next page

Beer-Braised Chuck Roast with Red Onions, Parsnips, and Carrots

» *Continued*

Sour Cream Smashed Potatoes

Prep time: 5 minutes • Cook time: 45 minutes • Yield: 4–6 servings

3–4 pounds (10–12) Yukon Gold potatoes

1 cup heavy cream (more, if needed)

1 cup sour cream

½ cup butter

½ cup milk

Salt and pepper to taste

Quarter the potatoes and place in a large pot, then cover with cool but not cold water. Bring water and potatoes to a rolling boil over high heat, then reduce to medium-high heat, bringing the water to a soft boil. Continue to cook over medium-high heat until the potatoes are easily pierced with a knife. Drain the potatoes, then add back to the pot. Add the cream, sour cream, butter, milk, salt, and pepper. Smash the potatoes using a handheld potato masher. The potatoes are done when the butter is melted and liquid is absorbed. They will be chunky.

Cheddar and Dill Baked Potato Soup

Prep time: 10 minutes • Cook time: 90 minutes • Yield: 4–6 servings

7–8 medium-sized Yukon gold potatoes

1 pound bacon, 8–10 thick-cut strips, roughly chopped (reserve ½ cup for garnish)

1 tablespoon butter

1 medium yellow onion, finely chopped

2 ribs celery, chopped

2 cloves fresh garlic, chopped

¼ cup all-purpose flour

4 cups chicken stock

2 cups heavy cream

Kosher salt and pepper to taste

2 cups shredded sharp cheddar cheese (reserve ½ cup for garnish)

½ cup chopped fresh dill, divided

½ cup diced green onions (for serving)

1 cup crème fraîche or sour cream (for serving)

PAIR WITH:

- *Beer & Grapefruit Spritzers (page 197)*

- *Short-Crust Sour Cherry Cobbler (page 148)*

- *Olive Oil and Espresso Dark Chocolate Cake with Cream Cheese Buttercream and Caramel (page 171)*

Preheat the oven to 350°. Bake the potatoes uncovered in a 9-by-13-inch pan with ¼ cup water for 1 hour. Remove and allow to cool. Cook the chopped bacon in the butter in a heavy-bottomed soup pot over medium heat until crisp and golden brown. Remove bacon and cook onion and celery in the fat. Add garlic, sauté 1 minute, then add flour. Whisk to create a roux. Cook 2 to 3 minutes, and slowly add stock and cream to the pan. Season with salt and pepper, and whisk until it begins to slightly thicken. Roughly chop the potatoes, skin included, and add to the creamy soup. Simmer soup 15 to 20 minutes, and add the bacon, cheese, and dill, setting some aside for serving. Stir until cheese is melted. Taste for seasoning and serve by garnishing with bacon, shredded cheddar cheese, the remaining dill, the green onions, and sour cream.

Bacon, Tomato, and Mushroom Campanelle with Spinach and Parmesan Salad

Bacon, Tomato, and Mushroom Campanelle

Prep time: 10 minutes • Cook time: 15 minutes • Yield: 4 servings

2 tablespoons olive oil

4–5 strips thick-cut peppered
bacon

1 cup diced yellow or red onion

2 cups halved cherry tomatoes

½ cup chopped flat leaf parsley

½ diced red chili

¼ teaspoon cracked black pepper

1 pinch crushed red pepper flakes

1 cup sliced brown mushrooms

2 cloves fresh garlic, crushed

Salt to taste

1 pound dried short pasta (we
chose campanelle), cooked al
dente according to package
instructions

1½ cups pasta water

3 tablespoons grated parmesan
or nutty hard cheese (we
found Herve Mon Abundonce
Fermiere; use this selection for
the salad as well)

PAIR WITH:

- *Cream Coconut Cake (page 156)*
- *Chocolate Almond Coconut Granola Sundae (page 166)*

Sauté the bacon and onion in the olive oil in a large skillet over medium to medium-high heat until the bacon renders most of its fat. Add the tomatoes, parsley, chili, pepper, pepper flakes, and salt to taste, then sauté for about a minute until the tomatoes give up some of their juices. Set aside 2 to 3 tablespoons of the liquid from the pan in a medium-sized bowl for the citronette. Add the mushrooms and garlic to the skillet. Sauté 2 to 3 minutes, and add the boiled pasta and pasta water. Cook for 5 minutes. Pour the pasta in a serving bowl, and add grated cheese over the top.

Spinach and Parmesan Salad

Prep time: 5 minutes • Yield: 4 servings

2–3 tablespoons reserved cooking
olive oil, bacon fat, and tomato
juice

2 tablespoons lemon juice

½ teaspoon honey

½ teaspoon mustard

Salt and pepper to taste

4 cups washed, chopped spinach

2 tablespoons grated cheese
(see above)

Add the lemon juice, honey, mustard, and salt and pepper to the reserved oil. Whisk to combine, and pour over fresh spinach leaves. Add grated cheese and serve.

Sausage and Leek Puff Pastry Pie with Baby Greens and Red Pesto Dressing

Sausage and Leek Puff Pastry Pie

Prep time: 30 minutes • Bake time: 20–25 minutes
Yield: 1 9×13-inch pie, 4–6 servings

1½ pounds sweet or mild loose Italian sausage

1 teaspoon olive oil

4 Yukon gold potatoes, diced

1 large leek, washed thoroughly and diced

2 cloves fresh garlic, chopped

1 young* bunch collard greens, ribs removed and chopped, roughly 3 cups

1 tablespoon butter

¼ cup all-purpose flour

Salt and pepper to taste

4 cups low-sodium chicken stock

1 cup heavy cream

½ cup grated parmesan cheese

1 box puff pastry, thawed in the refrigerator

1 egg, beaten with 1 tablespoon cool water

PAIR WITH:

- *Cinnamon Hot Chocolate (page 202), served alongside Noah's Apple Cake*

- *Noah's Apple Cake (page 175)*

- *One-Pan Lava Cake (page 175)*

* *Collard greens come in various-sized bunches during the season. Early in the season, some bunches will be young and no larger than 6 to 8 inches in diameter. As the season progresses, the leaves get larger. I prefer the smaller-sized leaves due to their tenderness, but larger leaves will work as well. Chop at least 3 cups of leaves.*

Preheat oven to 375°. Brown the sausage in olive oil for 6 to 7 minutes over medium to medium-high heat in a large, heavy-bottomed soup pot. Add the potatoes, leek, garlic, and collard greens. Cook 7 to 10 minutes until the greens have wilted and the potatoes begin to soften slightly. Add the butter and flour. Cook 2 to 3 minutes, until the flour has cooked through. Season with salt and pepper. Add the chicken stock, and lower heat to medium, then simmer 10 minutes, and stir in the cream and parmesan. Pour the contents into a 9-by-13-inch pan and top with 2 puff pastry crusts. They will overlap a bit. Pastry that is significantly under the other pastry will not puff. Using them in strips is great as well and allows for an even puff. Use a paring knife to make an X in the center of the pie for a steam vent. Brush the entire surface of the pastry with the beaten egg wash. Bake 20 to 25 minutes, until the pastry is puffed and golden. Allow to stand 10 minutes outside the oven before serving.

Recipe continues on next page

Continued

Greens and Red Pesto Dressing

Prep time: 10 minutes • Yield: 4–6 servings

1 jarred red pepper, fire roasted works, about ½ cup

½ cup flat leaf parsley

½ cup cilantro

1 clove fresh garlic

Juice of 1 lemon

⅓ cup shredded parmesan cheese

Salt and pepper to taste

½ cup olive oil

6–8 cups baby red romaine or green of your choice

To prepare the red pesto dressing, put the pepper, parsley, cilantro, garlic, lemon juice, parmesan, salt, and pepper in your food processor and blend. Once the mixture is chopped very small, spoon the contents into a large jar and add olive oil. Mix gently with a spoon. Keeps refrigerated for 1 week. Serve dressing over greens.

Tuscan Veggie and Chickpea Stew and Cheesy Scallion Soda Bread

Tuscan Veggie and Chickpea Stew

Prep time: 15 minutes • Cook time: 60 minutes • Yield: 6 servings

1 red onion, chopped

4–6 cloves fresh garlic, smashed

½ teaspoon cracked black pepper

¼ teaspoon crushed red pepper
flakes

¼ cup olive oil

3 ribs celery, chopped

2–3 carrots, sliced

1 red bell pepper, chopped

1 bunch lacinato kale (a.k.a.
Tuscan kale or dinosaur kale),
rinsed, chopped, ribs removed

2 tablespoons tomato paste

Kosher salt to taste

1 bunch flat leaf parsley leaves,
chopped

2 sprigs fresh lemon thyme

2 sprigs fresh rosemary

1 bay leaf

4 cups chicken or vegetable stock

2 (15-ounce) cans chickpeas or
garbanzo beans, drained

1 (15-ounce) can tomatoes in
juice

> **PAIR WITH:**
>
> • *Mom's Wine Punch (page 194)*
>
> • *Apple Cinnamon Monkey Bread (page 135)*

Sauté the onions, garlic, black pepper, and pepper flakes in olive oil in a large soup pot over medium heat. After 2 to 3 minutes, add celery, carrots, bell pepper, kale, and tomato paste. Season liberally with kosher salt. Sauté 3 to 4 minutes. Add the fresh herbs, stock, chickpeas, and canned tomatoes, then thin with water if necessary. Simmer over low heat 45 minutes to one hour. This stew tastes better the longer it cooks, so feel free to put it all into a slow cooker for the day or simmer on the stove for a few hours. Serve with a lemon wedge and a swirl of olive oil.

Cheesy Scallion Soda Bread

Prep time: 10 minutes • Cook time: 60 minutes • Resting time: 30 minutes • Yield: 1 16-ounce loaf

3½ cups all-purpose flour

1 teaspoon cracked black pepper

1 teaspoon baking soda

1 tablespoon baking powder

1 teaspoon salt

½ cup plus 2 tablespoons butter,
softened

1 cup shredded sharp cheddar
cheese

½ cup shredded parmesan cheese

1 cup diced scallions

1 cup heavy cream

¼ cup whole milk

1 egg

Preheat the oven to 350°. Mix the dry ingredients with the butter, cheeses, and scallions until crumbly. Add the wet ingredients, and mix until the dough has just come together. Turn the dough out onto a floured surface, and shape into a round. Transfer to a baking sheet, and slice an X for venting in the center. Bake for 60 minutes. Let cool for 30 minutes before slicing so the center can continue to bake once out of the oven.

Ground Beef Stroganoff with Parmesan Skillet Broccoli

Ground Beef Stroganoff

Prep time: 10 minutes • Cook time: 20 minutes • Yield: 4 servings

1½ pounds ground beef

1 red onion, diced

1 (16-ounce) package of
 mushrooms, sliced

Salt and pepper to taste

2 cloves fresh garlic, finely chopped

1½ cups heavy cream

1½ cups stock (beef or chicken)

¼ cup shredded parmesan cheese

½ cup diced flat leaf parsley

Cooked egg noodles for serving

PAIR WITH:

* *Beer and Grapefruit Spritzers (page 197)*
* *Apricot and Chocolate Rolls (page 151)*
* *Churros con Chocolate (page 168)*

TIP:

If sauce breaks, add a little flour slurry.

Brown the ground beef and onion in a large nonstick skillet over medium-high heat for 6 to 7 minutes, until beef is cooked through. Add the mushrooms, and season with salt and pepper. Add the garlic, and cook 1 to 2 minutes. Add the cream and stock, and reduce heat to medium. Cook 10 minutes. The cream will bubble and thicken (known as reducing your sauce). Remove from heat, and stir in the cheese and parsley. Serve over prepared egg noodles.

Parmesan Skillet Broccoli

Prep time: 10 minutes • Cook time: 10 minutes • Yield: 4–6 serving

1 medium yellow onion

1 tablespoon butter

1 tablespoon olive oil

1 pinch crushed red pepper flakes

3 whole broccoli crowns

2 cloves fresh garlic, chopped

Salt and pepper to taste

1 cup grated parmesan cheese

Sauté the onion in butter, oil, and pepper flakes in a large skillet over medium to medium-high heat. Slice the broccoli crowns as thinly as you can, almost shaved but not so much that it completely falls apart, and add to the pan. Cook until the broccoli begins to caramelize, along with the onions, but still has a crispy tenderness. Two minutes before broccoli is done, add the chopped garlic and season with salt and pepper. Cook just long enough that garlic becomes fragrant and has lost its raw bite, about 10 minutes. Toss with the grated parmesan and serve.

Steak "Dianna" with Creamy Cauliflower Mashed Potatoes and Stovetop Ratatouille

Steak "Dianna"

Prep time: 5 minutes • Cook time: 15 minutes • Yield: 4–6 servings

1 tablespoon butter

1 tablespoon olive oil

2 pounds tri-tip, or any steak you love, room temperature

Salt and pepper to taste

> **PAIR WITH:**
>
> • *Tender Gingerbread Cake (page 144)*
>
> • *Vanilla Panna Cotta with Citrus Caramel (page 147)*

Crack a window open, and heat a cast iron pan or nonstick pan over medium to medium-high heat. Melt the butter, and add the oil. Season the steaks generously with salt and pepper, and add to the pan. Turn the steaks every minute until a deep golden-brown, crisp crust develops. Do not crowd the pan; cook in 2 or 3 batches if necessary to ensure browning. Cook steaks to desired doneness; the time will depend on the thickness of the steaks. Remove the steaks from the pan, and set on a plate to rest.

Pan Sauce

Prep time: 10 minutes • Cook time: 5 minutes • Yield: 4–6 servings

½ cup diced shallots

1 clove fresh garlic, smashed

1 teaspoon Dijon mustard

1½ cups heavy cream

1 teaspoon of A.1. or your preference steak sauce

Resting juices from the steak

Salt and pepper to taste

Lower heat to medium-low. Add the shallots to the pan drippings, and sauté until tender, then add garlic and mustard and the juices from the steak resting on the plate. Cook for a minute or so. Add the cream and steak sauce, then reduce for 2 minutes. Season with salt and pepper, and serve over the steak and mashed cauliflower potatoes.

Recipe continues on next page

Continued

Cauliflower Mashed Potatoes

Prep time: 15 minutes • Cook time: 20 minutes • Yield: 4–6 servings

1 medium-sized head cauliflower, cut into florets

3 medium-sized Yukon gold potatoes, diced

1/2 cup butter

1 cup heavy cream

1/2 cup whole milk

2 tablespoons olive oil

Kosher salt and pepper to taste

Add cauliflower and potatoes to a large pot with just enough water to cover, and bring to a boil. Cook veggies until fork tender and mashable. Drain thoroughly and place back over medium heat. Add the butter, cream, and milk. Mash using a hand masher until you've reached your desired texture (my family loves it a bit chunky). Season generously with kosher salt and pepper.

Stovetop Ratatouille

Prep time: 10 minutes • Cook time: 20 minutes • Yield: 4 servings

1 red onion, peeled and sliced

2 zucchini, sliced into thin coins

2 cups ripe cherry tomatoes

¼–½ cup olive oil

1 pinch crushed red pepper flakes

2 cloves fresh garlic, chopped

Sauté the onion in the olive oil in a large nonstick skillet over medium to medium-high heat until it begins to caramelize. Add the zucchini and tomatoes, and season with salt, pepper, and pepper flakes. Cook for 8 to 10 minutes, until the tomatoes have burst and the zucchini is tender and falling apart. Add the garlic for the final 2 minutes of cooking. This lends a bright garlic flavor to the soft vegetables.

Pistachio-Crusted Chicken Cutlets with Simple Heirloom Tomato and Ricotta Salad

Pistachio-Crusted Chicken Cutlets

Prep time: 10 minutes • Cook time: 20 minutes • Yield: 4 servings

PAIR WITH:

- *Strawberry Bellini (page 209)*
- *Cherry Pie Bars (page 136)*

CRUST

½ cup crushed pistachios

½ cup grated parmesan cheese

¼ cup fresh basil leaves

2 cups panko bread crumbs

1 teaspoon garlic powder

1 teaspoon onion powder

1 pinch crushed red pepper flakes

Salt and pepper to taste

FLOUR DREDGE

2 cups all-purpose flour

EGG WASH

2 eggs

CHICKEN

4 chicken breasts, sliced in half to make 8 thin cutlets, seasoned liberally with salt and pepper

2 tablespoons butter

2 tablespoons olive oil

Pulse the pistachios, cheese, and basil in the bowl of a food processor until finely chopped. Pour mixture into a large, shallow bowl, and add bread crumbs, seasonings, salt, and pepper. Mix well. Set up a breading station with 3 large, shallow bowls. Fill the first with flour, the second with beaten eggs, and the third with pistachio bread crumbs.

Dredge seasoned chicken in the flour and shake off excess. Dip flour-coated chicken into beaten egg, then press each side of the chicken into bread crumbs. Repeat this process until you've coated all your chicken.

Meanwhile, heat a large skillet with high sides over medium heat. Melt butter and olive oil, then add breaded chicken cutlets. Fry 3 to 4 cutlets at a time for 3 to 4 minutes per side. Nuts can burn very quickly. Take care in not overheating the pan. Lower the temperature if chicken is cooking too quickly or getting too brown. Top with heirloom tomato salad.

Recipe continues on next page

— *Continued*

Heirloom Tomato and Ricotta Salad
Prep time: 5 minutes • Yield: 4 servings

2–3 large heirloom slicing tomatoes

¼ cup olive oil

½ cup sliced basil

Salt and pepper to taste

6 ounces ricotta cheese

Slice tomatoes into roughly half-inch cubes. Toss with olive oil, basil, salt, and pepper. Spoon tomato mixture over cooked chicken in a large serving tray, and dot ricotta over top of the mixture.

FOR FRIENDSHIP + COMPANY   33

For Comfort + Family

The most important work you'll ever do is within your home.

The way the sunlight poured through the dusty windows of the turn-of-the-twentieth-century military school was magical. Those windows looked clean on cloudy days and smeared on bright ones. Our small, nondenominational church congregation—about 150 members strong in our heyday—met there every Sunday and Wednesday to worship. I can still see my mother, and all the other mothers who went there, with hands raised. I can still hear the little makeshift church band, complete with guitar, tambourine, and piano, warming up for a hopeful Sunday. Members of the congregation would take turns with coffee service and after-church snacks—Styrofoam cups, tiny wooden stir sticks, packets of Sweet'N Low. I can still smell that coffee brewing in the lobby, and I can see kids being scolded for grabbing too many sugar packets and stir sticks. I always felt so special getting my cup of coffee before church. That smell of old wood and coffee brewing in a pot will never leave me; it makes me think of Sundays. Large, creaking, wooden doors revealed the entrance to the little sanctuary. We'd hear a word about God's purpose in our lives and sing songs and head down to "kids church" for crafts and snacks. My siblings and I would run the halls of the school while our parents visited after service. The single greatest thing my mother ever did for me as a child was take me to church. I long for the days of my childhood church.

The lessons I learned about Jesus and community run very deep. Church potlucks were a smorgasbord of unusual foods, some delicious and some exceptionally bad. We kids would explore the back pantries in the cafeteria when setting up for the weekend meal, where every family in the church eagerly brought food to share. I learned what gumbo was at one of these potlucks, and it was glorious! Bits of okra and spicy sausage, or sometimes shrimp or crab. In every case, it was exotic and wonderful! This was where I began to understand the value of sharing. Church was a lesson in home. These people became part of your family. The women's fellowship—all of eight to ten ladies—would gather at a local place that was part diner, part café, dark and smoky inside, with a pie turnstile. They served bumbleberry cobblers and French dip sandwiches with cheddar cheese. This place felt like such a treat for me. I was maybe eleven, but the women's fellowship made me feel like an adult. We'd sit around a long table and just visit. It was this wonderful break from being a child. I'd take it all in, hardly talking, just feeling special to be part of something. *This* was what women did! They ordered dessert and discussed *life*. To be welcomed into this sort of secret society, if you will, was my first taste of community. To this day, I enjoy being in a group of ladies, particularly at a restaurant.

As I got older, I began asking my mom if I could please just stay home from church. An angsty teen, I figured I had far better things to do than hang about the church halls. But what I didn't realize was that every Sunday, a brick was being laid in my foundation, and I was being built into who I am today.

These days, I find myself longing for that same sense of community I often complained about in our little church. I realize now that the friends I had there, the lessons I learned about community and kindness, and the memories I made were precious. I had no idea I'd unknowingly draw upon my childhood church experience throughout my adult life and with my very own husband and children. The songs I learned then I still sing to my boys almost nightly: "God Will Make a Way" and "I Have a Constant Friend." I believe very strongly that a small community where people truly care for one other is attainable for everybody if we just allow our homes and hearts to be open enough to let people in and feed them. And you don't need an arsenal of exotic, new dishes to grace the table nightly. Repetition can be a good thing. You just need wholesome food your kids find comfort in.

We really share first with our families. My favorite quote, and I've said it before, is "The most important work we will ever do is in our home." Your family are the people you see the most and spend the most time with. There is no kind of comfort like that found in a family. My hope is that you also find comfort in the meals in this section.

36 FOR COMFORT + FAMILY

Creamy Sausage and Mushroom Lasagna and Boston Buttermilk Salad

Creamy Sausage and Mushroom Lasagna

Prep time: 10 minutes • Cook time: 65 minutes • Yield: 1 9×13-inch pan, feeds 4–6 people generously

FILLING

2 pounds mushrooms*

1 tablespoon olive oil

1 pound ground country-style pork sausage

1 medium onion, diced

2 cloves fresh garlic, smashed

GARLIC AND PARMESAN BÉCHAMEL

2–3 tablespoons butter

Salt and pepper to taste

1 pinch crushed red pepper flakes

4 cloves fresh garlic, smashed

¼ cup all-purpose flour

5 cups whole milk

1 cup shredded parmesan cheese

LASAGNA

3 cups shredded mozzarella cheese

1 cup whole milk ricotta cheese

1 (10-ounce) package fresh pasta lasagna noodles**

1 loose cup torn basil leaves, roughly 10–12 leaves

PAIR WITH:

- *Chocolate Chip Pumpkin Bread (page 152)*

- *Pumpkin Tiramisu (page 143)*

....

*   *Feel free to use any type of mushroom. Button or cremini work great. We used oyster, which give a meaty flavor.*

**   *If you can't find fresh pasta at your grocer and you don't feel like making it, feel free to boil dried lasagna pasta sheets according to package instructions. Or use no-bake lasagna noodles.*

***   *This process is known as making a roux.*

Preheat oven to 350°. Sauté the mushrooms in olive oil in a large skillet until they begin to caramelize slightly, 3 to 4 minutes. Add the sausage, onion, and garlic, and brown until fully cooked, about 7 to 8 minutes. Set aside.

To make the béchamel, melt the butter with the salt, pepper, red pepper flakes, and garlic in a large, heavy-bottomed saucepan over medium heat until the butter begins to get foamy. Add the flour and stir to make a paste***. Cook 2 to 3 minutes. Slowly pour in milk one cup at a time, whisking after each addition to make sure milk is completely mixed into the roux. Simmer over low heat for 9 to 10 minutes, until thickened. Remove from heat and add the cheese. Stir to melt the cheese.

To assemble the lasagna, pour 1 cup of the prepared béchamel along the bottom of a 9-by-13-inch pan. Lay enough noodles down to cover the bottom of the pan. Sprinkle half of meat mixture over

Recipe continues on next page

» Continued

the noodles, then one-third of the remaining béchamel sauce, 1 cup shredded mozzarella, and ½ cup ricotta (dotted on top). Cover with more pasta sheets and repeat this process with the last of the sausage, second third of the sauce, and 1 cup shredded mozzarella. For third and final layer, lay the noodles over top of sausage and cheese, pour final third of sauce over the top, and cover with the last of the mozzarella (roughly 1 cup). Cover the lasagna tightly with foil. Bake 35 to 45 minutes, removing foil for last 10 minutes of cooking. Allow to stand 15 to 20 minutes before slicing and serving.

Boston Buttermilk Salad

Prep time: 10 minutes • Yield: 4–6 servings

This is my favorite old-school Italian American salad recipe. Perfect for the lasagna!

DRESSING

½ cup full-fat buttermilk

2 tablespoons olive oil

1 teaspoon onion powder

1 clove fresh garlic, smashed and
  minced

½ teaspoon dried oregano

½ teaspoon black pepper

Salt to taste

SALAD

2 heads Boston or red leaf lettuce

1 cup cherry tomatoes, sliced

1 (15-ounce) can sliced black
  olives

1½ cups shredded mozzarella
  cheese

Combine all the dressing ingredients in a large mixing bowl. Whisk and let stand 15 minutes. When time to serve, place all the salad components on top of the dressing in the bowl. Toss gently just before serving. Feel free to serve the dressing on the side; this way, the lettuce will remain crisper.

Lydia's Casserole (Creamy Celery, Leek, Potato, and Kielbasa Sausage Bake) with Mixed Greens and Lemony Honey Mustard

Sweet and sour meatballs using grape jelly and ground pork? Hot dish? Monster cookies with butter-flavored Crisco? Kielbasa sausages cooked in condensed creamy celery soup and red potatoes? I had never heard of such food until I had the sweetest and most hospitable roommate, Lydia.

You know how every so often, you will meet someone who is just the salt of the earth, the kind of person who never gossips and wears warmth all over them? That was Lydia. Lydia worked in the nursing field, and she was as beautiful as she was gracious. Her family had a pig farm in Ohio, and she taught me so much about life. I, on the other hand, wasn't as kind at this time in my life. I was in my early twenties and more concerned with myself, how I felt, and my own opinions than I was with others. I mean, I always considered myself caring, but I thought I was right about most everything. I have long since forgiven the girl I was and am grateful I learned so much from the old me as well.

I'd come home from work, and Lydia would be making dinner or cookies or crumbles. She cooked very differently from how I ate growing up, and I loved it. It was true Midwestern comfort food. She had a boyfriend who liked to stay over more than I thought he ought to, so it began to drive a little wedge into our friendship. But she continued to cook dinner for our little piecemeal family and do it with a real smile.

One evening, I came home starving. Often, Lydia would write her name on her and her boyfriend's lunch, and for me, she'd leave a little container of whatever she'd made for dinner! On this particular evening, it was about 11:00 p.m., and I was just praying she'd left me something. Well, she happened to have made my favorite creamy potato and kielbasa sausage casserole. To my dismay, it must have been a small batch, because the tiny container I was used to finding for me wasn't there. There was one container, and it was labeled "Lydia." I stood in the dark kitchen, contemplating by the light of the fridge if I could have just a small bite. She'd never know, I reasoned. It's so late…maybe just a tiny bite?

WHO WAS I? This was not my food! Twenty-two-year-old Danielle did some things I look back on and think *WOOOOW*. I took the bite; I picked out a hunk of sausage, then another. It took all of three minutes for me to eat all the sausages in her lunch. Panic set in! *What do I do? I thought. Do I tell her? Do I eat all the potatoes? Do I run to the store, buy a sausage rope, and attempt to remake it? No, I'll just go to bed and pray to God in Heaven that she doesn't notice.*

The next morning around ten, I received a text message from Lydia. Should I open it? Should I pretend she isn't asking me where the meat in her lunch is?

"Hi, Danielle, weird question. Did you eat the sausage out of my lunch?"

Continued

Knee-jerk: "No, why?" That was my reaction! NO? WHY? *Danielle*, I thought, *this is VERY out of character for you. This is terrible. Tell the woman you ate them! She knows!* I said, "Maybe it was Mykayla?" We both knew it wasn't Mykayla. Mykayla, our other roommate, hadn't been home in a week.

Kind, sweet Lydia didn't press it. In fact, she continued to leave me food, and she didn't stop leaving me food until she moved away. She bought me a robe and flowers when I lost my job. She made cookies for our neighbors and never asked me about what happened to her lunch after that day. We continued to be roommates for another six to eight months or so.

I did not know how powerful an influence on my life Lydia was until years later. Lydia taught me to share, taught me how to love others even when they behave wrongly or eat all the good parts out of your leftovers. She kept no record of my wrongs, and I am very grateful for her. I didn't talk to Lydia much after she moved away and got married. I heard she moved back to Ohio and has a beautiful family. It's been about fifteen years since the lunch incident, and I think she'd be happy to know I've done some growing in that time.

So there you have it, Lydia. I ate your lunch and lied about it. I'm not sure what got into me, and I'm glad I didn't choose a life of crime because I don't think I could have made a go of it very well! I know you've forgiven me. Here is a recipe for your glorious, gloriously creamy sausage and potato bake. I've ditched the canned soup and added a few things. When I make this recipe, I am reminded of the day I ate all the sausage from Lydia's lunch, and in equal measure, I am reminded that grace is very real.

Lydia's Casserole (Creamy Celery, Leek, Potato, and Kielbasa Sausage Bake)

Prep time: 20 minutes • Bake time: 40 minutes • Yield: 4–6 servings

6 medium-sized red potatoes

1 cup finely diced white onion

2 cloves fresh garlic, smashed

2–3 tablespoons olive oil

2 tablespoons butter

1½ pounds kielbasa sausage, sliced

4 ribs celery, preferably with leaves, sliced on the bias

1 leek, cleaned and sliced*

¼ cup all-purpose flour

4 cups chicken stock

2 cups cream

Salt and pepper to taste

1 cup grated parmesan cheese

> **PAIR WITH:**
>
> • *Pineapple Cloud Cake (page 155)*
>
> • *Wild Dried Blueberry Pound Cake (page 167)*

* *Leeks are often sandy, so a soak in cool water can minimize stuck-on grit.*

Recipe continues on next page

» Continued

Preheat oven to 350° and butter a deep 9-by-13-inch casserole dish. Parboil the red potatoes 15 minutes in salted water. Drain, set aside, and once cool, slice into thin rounds. Sauté the onion and garlic over medium heat in the olive oil and butter and cook for 2 to 3 minutes. Add the sausage, celery, and leek, and cook for another 3 to 4 minutes. Evenly sprinkle the flour over the mixture, stir, and cook for another 3 to 4 minutes. Carefully add the stock and cream. Bring to a simmer to thicken. Add the sliced potatoes and season with salt and pepper. Pour the casserole into the prepared casserole dish. Cover tightly in foil and bake at least 30 minutes or until the potatoes are tender. Remove foil and sprinkle with parmesan cheese. Bake uncovered an additional 10 minutes to melt the cheese and crisp the edges of the casserole.

Mixed Greens and Lemony Honey Mustard

Prep time: 5 minutes • Yield: 1 cup dressing

½ cup mayonnaise

Juice of 1 lemon

1½ tablespoon yellow mustard

1 tablespoon honey

1 tablespoon spicy brown mustard

½ teaspoon cracked black pepper

1 teaspoon dried chives or 1 tablespoon fresh chives

¼ teaspoon garlic powder

¼ teaspoon onion powder

Kosher salt to taste

4–6 cups mixed greens

Mix all ingredients except mixed greens, and refrigerate two hours or up to overnight before serving. Serve dressing with your favorite mixed greens. This dressing is best made the day before. It will last one week in the refrigerator.

Chimichurri Chicken Meatballs with Herbed Greek Yogurt, Red Quinoa, and Green Beans

Herbed Greek Yogurt

Prep Time: 5 minutes • Yield: 4–6 servings

1½ cups whole milk plain Greek
  yogurt

Juice of 1 small lime

¼ cup cilantro leaves

¼ cup green onion tops

¼ cup Italian flat leaf parsley leaves

3–4 fresh basil leaves

1 clove fresh garlic

1 teaspoon onion powder

Salt and pepper to taste

> **PAIR WITH:**
> - *Mom's Wine Punch (page 194)*
> - *Apple Butter Crumb Cake (page 179)*

Pulse all the ingredients in the bowl of a food processor. Mix for 2 to 3 minutes or until you get the consistency you desire. We like ours pretty smooth. Transfer to a bowl and refrigerate until ready to use.

Quinoa

Prep Time: 5 minutes • Cook Time: 15 minutes • Yield: 4–6 servings

2 cups chicken stock

1 cup red quinoa

½ cup diced onion

Make the quinoa according to the package instructions, add the onion, and sub chicken stock for water, if you've got it.

Chimichurri Chicken Meatballs

Prep time: 10 minutes • Cook time: 20 minutes • Yield: 20–25 ½-ounce meatballs

6 boneless skinless chicken
  thighs (about 1½ pounds)

½ cup cilantro

½ cup Italian flat leaf parsley

½ small to medium yellow onion

¼ cup green onion tops

¼ cup pretzel crumbs

3–4 basil leaves

1 tablespoon fresh lime juice
  (hefty squeeze from ½ a lime)

1 egg

1 clove fresh garlic

Salt and pepper to taste

Recipe continues on next page

Chimichurri Chicken Meatballs with Herbed Greek Yogurt, Red Quinoa, and Green Beans

Continued

Slice the chicken thighs into thirds. Do not remove fat. Add all ingredients to the bowl of your food processor. Take care to evenly distribute items in order to pulse the mixer less. Pulse the mixer several times to break up and chop the meat. Mix until you've got a coarse paste. This mixture is very sticky. Use a small ½-ounce self-release ice cream scoop to portion—your hands work as well.

Heat 2 tablespoons olive oil over medium heat. Fry the meatballs for 6 to 8 minutes, gently turning them constantly to keep their round shape. Do this in 3 batches if you don't have a large enough pan. Don't crowd your pan or they won't caramelize.

Green Beans

Prep Time: 5 minutes • Cook Time: 4–6 minutes • Yield: 4–6 servings

1 tablespoon olive oil

1 pound fresh green beans, trimmed and cut

2 cloves fresh garlic, chopped

Salt and pepper to taste

Sauté the green beans in olive oil for 2 to 3 minutes over medium-high heat. Add 2 tablespoons water, and cook with the lid on for another 2 to 3 minutes. Remove the lid and add the garlic, salt, and pepper. To serve, layer quinoa, green beans, and meatballs in a bowl, then top with yogurt.

Baked Salmon with Strawberry Basil Relish and Herb and Parmesan Israeli Couscous

Baked Salmon with Strawberry Basil Relish

Prep time: 10 minutes • Cook time: 10–15 minutes • Yield: 4 servings

PAIR WITH:

- *Strawberry Bellini (page 209)*
- *Creamy Lime Tart (page 159)*

BAKED SALMON

2–2½ pounds wild salmon

1 teaspoon olive oil

Salt and pepper to taste

STRAWBERRY BASIL RELISH

2 cups halved, chopped fresh strawberries

¼ cup olive oil

½ cup chopped fresh basil

½ lemon

Salt and pepper to taste

Preheat oven to 350° and line a quarter sheet baking pan with parchment paper. Place salmon on the paper and rub with olive oil. Season with salt and pepper, and bake 10 to 15 minutes or until salmon is cooked through but not overdone. It should flake easily. Meanwhile, mix ingredients for the strawberry relish, except for the lemon. Top salmon with the relish, and squeeze lemon all over the fish. Serve warm or room temperature.

Herb and Parmesan Israeli Couscous

Prep time: 15 minutes • Yield: 4 servings

1½ cups low-sodium stock or water

1 teaspoon olive oil

¼ teaspoon kosher salt

1 cup Israeli or large pearl couscous

½ cup roughly chopped fresh basil

½ cup chopped fresh flat leaf parsley

¼ cup chopped fresh dill

Juice of ½ lemon

½ cup shredded parmesan cheese

¼ cup olive oil

Salt and pepper to taste

Bring the stock or water, olive oil, and salt to a boil, then add the couscous. Cover and reduce heat to low. Cook 10 minutes. Place the cooked pasta on a plate to cool for 5 minutes, then add the warm couscous to a mixing bowl and top with the herbs, lemon juice, cheese, olive oil, and salt and pepper. Gently toss and serve.

Quick Creole Shrimp Étouffée with Butter Lettuce and Mushroom Salad

This recipe has some wonderful traditional elements and some very fun shortcuts! I know the golden roux is the cornerstone of all great Creole cooking, but sometimes when adapting recipes to fit our busy schedules, it's important to try a different method. I skip the roux base altogether and swap it out for thickened cream. The gulf shrimp I picked up are plump and juicy, and this entire dish comes together in the time it takes to cook the rice, with just a little prep!

Quick Creole Shrimp Étouffée

Prep time: 10 minutes • Cook time: 20 minutes • Yield: 4 servings

2 tablespoons butter

2 tablespoons olive oil

1 teaspoon ground paprika

1½–2 pounds gulf shrimp, peeled and deveined

Kosher salt to taste (be sure to season every step of the sauce)

1 teaspoon onion powder

½ teaspoon garlic powder

½ teaspoon cracked black pepper

¼ teaspoon ground chili powder

¼ teaspoon ground white pepper

1 pinch crushed red pepper flakes

1 pinch ground cayenne pepper

4 cloves fresh garlic

2 shallots, finely chopped

1 green bell pepper, one half sliced, one half diced

1 red bell pepper, one half sliced, one half diced

¾ cup chopped celery

3 cups heavy cream

½ cup chopped flat leaf parsley, divided

1 cup chopped green onions or scallions

4–5 cups cooked jasmine rice

> **PAIR WITH:**
> - *Virgin Mary Mix (page 201)*
> - *Magic Shell and Pistachio Sundae (page 162)*

* *Make sure shrimp are peeled, deveined, rinsed, then patted dry.*

Melt the butter into the olive oil in a large skillet over medium to medium-high heat. Add the paprika to the hot butter and oil. Once foamy, add the shrimp. Do this in 2 batches, so the shrimp cook evenly and don't steam, losing their juices. Sauté the shrimp for 1 minute on each side*. Season with kosher salt. The shrimp will not be quite cooked through, but remove them and set aside. Add the rest of your seasoning to the hot pan, then add the garlic, shallots, diced bell peppers, and celery. Season all this with kosher salt. Allow the veggies to cook 2 to 3 minutes, then add the heavy cream. Allow the cream to begin to bubble around the edges of the pan. Cook 2 to 3 minutes, then taste for seasoning, according to taste. Add the shrimp and sliced peppers to the dish along with ¼ cup parsley. Cook shrimp in the hot, bubbling cream 3 to 4 minutes until cooked through and bell peppers are crisp tender. Serve over steamed jasmine rice and garnish with the remainder of fresh parsley and chopped scallions.

Recipe continues on next page

Continued

Butter Lettuce and Mushroom Salad

Prep time: 10 minutes • Yield: 4–6 servings

VINAIGRETTE

⅓ cup olive oil

⅓ cup white or champagne
vinegar

1 teaspoon dried oregano

½ teaspoon ground black pepper

1 teaspoon granulated sugar

Sea salt to taste

SALAD

2 heads butter lettuce, washed
and core removed

1 pound button mushrooms,
thinly sliced

1 bunch green onions, thinly
sliced

½ cup toasted sliced almonds

Whisk vinaigrette ingredients in a bowl and set aside. Layer the lettuce leaves with the mushrooms, green onions, and sliced almonds. Spoon the dressing over the salad just before serving. The vinegar will wilt the lettuce if dressed early. You will not need all the dressing; it stores nicely up to 10 days in the fridge.

Enchilada Meatballs (Albondigas) with Spanish Rice and Refried Beans

Enchilada Meatballs (Albondigas)

Prep time: 15 minutes • Cook time: 20–30 minutes • Yield: 14–16 1-ounce meatballs

1 slice sandwich bread (sub ¼ cup almond flour for keto or Whole30 preparation)

1 pound ground beef or turkey

1 egg

1 teaspoon ground chili powder

1 teaspoon onion powder

1 clove fresh garlic, crushed

Salt and pepper to taste

2 tablespoons olive oil

2 cups prepared enchilada sauce (recipe below)

1 cup shredded cheddar cheese (as garnish)*

> **PAIR WITH:**
> * *Cinnamon Hot Chocolate with Soft Whipped Cream (page 202)*
> * *Churros con Chocolate (page 168)*

* *Cheese is not included on the Whole30 diet plan and may be omitted from recipe.*

Pulse bread in the bowl of your food processor to make a fine crumb. Combine the crumbs, beef or turkey, egg, seasonings, and garlic in a mixing bowl, and mix well with a fork. Shape meat into balls a bit larger than a tablespoon. Sauté in olive oil over medium heat in a large nonstick frying pan. Once the balls are set but not cooked through, add enchilada sauce, and simmer for 5 to 10 minutes over low heat. When meatballs are ready, cover in cheese and serve with rice or veggies.

Enchilada Sauce

Cook time 30 minutes • Yields 2 quarts of sauce

2 tablespoons olive oil

1 large yellow onion

6 dried Ancho chilies

6 dried California chilies

6 dried Guajillo chilies

2–3 Arbol chilies (optional, these chilies add heat)

2 cloves fresh garlic

Salt and pepper to taste

5 cups low-sodium chicken stock

1 (28-ounce) can crushed tomatoes

Sauté onion in olive oil in a large saucepan over medium heat until it begins to caramelize. Add dried chilies with seeds and stems removed. Sauté 2 to 3 minutes and add garlic. Continue cooking until garlic becomes fragrant. Season with salt and pepper. Add chicken stock and tomatoes, and bring to a boil. Turn off heat, cover pot with a lid, and allow chilies to steep for 20 minutes. Blend the mixture with a stick blender or in your standard blender. Bring enchilada sauce to a boil again and taste for seasoning. Add salt and pepper. If the sauce is thicker than you'd like, add a bit more chicken stock or water to thin. This sauce packs a mild heat and has a rich smoky flavor.

» Recipe continues on next page

Enchilada Meatballs (Albondigas) with Spanish Rice and Refried Beans

Continued

Refried Beans

Prep time: 20 minutes • Cook time: 1 hour • Yield: 4 servings

¼ pound pork belly, diced

1 medium yellow onion, diced

1 green bell pepper, diced

1 red bell pepper, diced

1 medium-sized jalapeño, seeded and diced

½ cup neutral oil such as canola or light olive oil

2 tablespoons butter

3 (15-ounce) cans of pinto beans, drained

Salt and pepper to taste

Sauté the pork belly, onion, peppers, and jalapeño in oil and butter in a large, heavy-bottomed pan until onions are soft and translucent and pork is rendered but nothing has browned too much. Add the beans and smash with a potato masher, then mix into pork and vegetables. Season with salt and pepper, and simmer covered over low for one hour, stirring often so beans do not stick. Beans should be creamy and loose when finished cooking.

Spanish Rice

Prep time: 10 minutes • Cook time: 30 minutes • Yield: 4 servings

1 medium yellow onion, finely chopped

1 tablespoon olive oil

1 tablespoon tomato paste

1 teaspoon ground cumin

1 teaspoon onion powder

1 teaspoon ground chili powder

½ teaspoon ground turmeric

Salt and pepper to taste

2 cups jasmine rice

2 cloves fresh garlic, finely chopped

4 cups low-sodium chicken stock or broth

½ cup chopped cilantro

½ cup chopped green onions

Juice of 1 lime

Sweat the onion in the olive oil over medium heat 3 to 4 minutes in a medium-sized pot with lid, taking care not to brown onion. Add the tomato paste, cumin, onion powder, chili powder, turmeric, and salt and pepper, then cook another 2 to 3 minutes. Add the jasmine rice and garlic to the pan, cooking additional 1 to 2 minutes. Add the chicken stock and increase heat to high. Bring to a boil, then reduce heat to low and cover. Cook 15 to 20 minutes on low heat. Fluff with a fork and remove from heat once finished cooking. Mix in the fresh cilantro and green onions and lime juice.

Sweet 'n' Sour Chicken with Cheap Chow Mein

Sweet 'n' Sour Chicken

Prep time: 10 minutes • Cook time: 20 minutes • Yield: 10 servings

CHICKEN

4 cups vegetable oil (for frying the chicken)

10–12 boneless, skinless chicken thighs, cut into bite-sized pieces

2–3 tablespoons soy sauce

Salt and pepper to taste

BATTER

2½ cups seltzer water (we used lemon lime)

2 cups all-purpose flour

3 teaspoons kosher salt

PAIR WITH:

- *Beer and Grapefruit Spritzers (page 197)*

- *Pear Brandy (page 195), served alongside Noah's Apple Cake*

- *Noah's Apple Cake (page 175)*

Heat the oil in a heavy-bottomed skillet to roughly 325°. It will shimmer but not smoke. Season the chicken with the soy sauce, salt, and pepper, and set aside. Mix the batter ingredients in a large bowl. Place one-quarter of the chicken into the batter, then drop each piece into the hot oil. Fry for 7 to 10 minutes or until the chicken is cooked completely—this time varies depending on how hot the oil is and how big the chicken pieces are. Repeat with the rest of the chicken. Cover with prepared sweet 'n' sour sauce and serve alongside chow mein.

Sweet 'n' Sour Sauce

Prep Time: 5 minutes • Cook Time: 13 minutes • Yield: 10 servings

2 cups pineapple juice

¼ cup ketchup

¼ cup soy sauce

⅓ cup rice vinegar

2 tablespoons dark brown sugar

1 clove fresh garlic, crushed

1 teaspoon kosher salt

1 teaspoon toasted chili sesame oil

½ teaspoon cracked black pepper

2 heaping teaspoons cornstarch

Combine all the ingredients except the cornstarch in a medium-sized saucepan, and bring to a boil. Whisk the cornstarch with ¼ cup cold water in a measuring cup, then whisk into the sauce. Turn heat down to low and simmer for 10 minutes or until the sauce thickens slightly and has taken on a glossy sheen.

Recipe continues on next page

Continued

Chow Mein Noodles

Prep Time: 15 minutes • Cook Time: 15 minutes • Yield: 10 servings

16 ounces spaghetti noodles,
cooked al dente according to
the package directions

2 cups chopped celery

1 medium yellow onion, sliced

1 bunch green onions, chopped

½ head green cabbage

½ cup rice vinegar

¼ cup olive oil

¼ cup sesame seeds

¼ cup soy sauce

2 tablespoons brown sugar

2 tablespoons yellow mustard

3 cloves fresh garlic, chopped

Salt and pepper to taste

Cook the noodles according to the package directions for al dente. They should have a bite to them.

Sauté the vegetables over medium-high heat in half the olive oil in a large skillet with high sides until they are crisp tender, 3 to 4 minutes. Add the cooked pasta and the remaining ingredients, including the oil, and cook 3 to 4 minutes, tossing frequently to mix the sauce right in the pan. Once the noodles are glossy and evenly coated with sauce, it's time to serve.

Pesto and Mozzarella Pasta with Italian Rocket and Chicken Salad

Pesto and Mozzarella Pasta

Prep time: 15 minutes • Cook time: 10–12 minutes • Yield: 4–6 servings

PESTO

3 cups baby spinach

1 cup fresh, sweet basil leaves

¾ cup olive oil

½ cup grated parmesan cheese

1 clove fresh garlic

Juice and zest of 1 lemon

Salt and pepper to taste

MOZZARELLA PASTA

12 ounces dry, short pasta, cooked according to package instructions

3 cups baby spinach leaves

2 cups miniature mozzarella balls (bocconcini)

1 cup cherry tomatoes, halved

Juice of 1 lemon

1 teaspoon garlic powder

Salt and pepper to taste

PAIR WITH:

- *Mom's Wine Punch (page 194)*

- *Cherry Pie Bars (page 136)*

- *Tender Gingerbread Cake (page 144)*

Whirl all the pesto ingredients in a food processor. Using the pulse option yields a pesto that retains some texture and won't be overly smooth. Refrigerate and use within 3 days. Cook the pasta and set aside to cool slightly. Combine all the pasta ingredients in a large bowl, then stir in the pesto. This pasta salad can be eaten right away warm or chilled.

Recipe continues on next page

Continued

Italian Rocket and Chicken Salad

Prep time: 15 minutes • Yield: 4–6 servings

DRESSING

1 cup olive oil

½ cup cilantro

½ cup fresh flat leaf parsley

Juice of 1 lemon

1 clove fresh garlic

½ teaspoon dried oregano

¼ teaspoon crushed red pepper
   flakes

¼ teaspoon ground cayenne pepper

Salt and pepper to taste

CHICKEN SALAD

6 cups young rocket (baby
   arugula)

3 cups prepared shredded chicken
   (rotisserie breasts work great)

1 cup dried cranberries

1 cup marinated artichoke hearts

1 cup slivered almonds

½ cup diced sun-dried tomatoes
   in oil

Place all dressing ingredients into a food processor or high-speed blender and pulse until dressing is thoroughly combined. You can finely chop and whisk by hand as well. Set aside.

Place all the salad ingredients in a large salad bowl. Add half the dressing and toss, and reserve the rest to spoon over individual portions.

Boneless Braised Pork Spareribs with Garlicky Chanterelles and Spaetzle

Boneless Braised Pork Spareribs

Prep time: 20 minutes • Inactive cook time: 4–6 hours • Cook time: 15 minutes
Yield: 8–10 servings

4 pounds boneless country-style
   spareribs
2 tablespoons olive oil
2 yellow onions, sliced
2 bay leaves
6 cloves fresh garlic, smashed
3 teaspoons kosher salt

1½ teaspoons cracked black
   pepper
1 (16-ounce) package spaetzle
   or short-cut egg pasta, cooked
   according to package directions

> **PAIR WITH:**
> - *Cream Coconut Cake (page 156)*
> - *Creamy Lime Tart (page 159)*

Preheat oven to 300°. Brown the pork in olive oil in a heavy-bottomed pan suitable for braising (think Dutch oven or similar vessel). Add the onions, bay leaves, garlic, salt, pepper, and 1 cup water. Place the lid on the pot and bake 4 to 6 hours, until the onions have nearly melted and meat can be cut with a fork. Serve with the cooked pasta, spooning meat, pan juices, and garlicky chanterelles over the top.

Garlicky Chanterelles

Prep time: 10 minutes • Cook Time: 7–10 minutes • Yield: 8–10 servings

1 pound fresh chanterelles*
2 tablespoons butter
2 tablespoons olive oil
1 yellow onion, sliced

1 pinch crushed red pepper
   flakes
Salt and pepper to taste
3 cloves fresh garlic, chopped

> * *Chanterelles are usually expensive. I found them for only $9.99 per pound on special. If you cannot find them at an affordable price, any mushroom will do.*

Sauté mushrooms in butter and olive oil in a sauté pan over medium to medium-high heat. Add onion, pepper flakes, and salt and pepper. Sauté 7 to 10 minutes, until the onions and mushrooms have caramelized. To keep garlic flavor bright, add the garlic during last five minutes of cooking.

Shrimp and Chive Penne and Garlic Knots

Shrimp and Chive Penne

Prep time: 10 minutes • Cook time: 15 minutes • Yield: 4–6 servings

16 ounces dry penne pasta

1½ pounds shrimp, peeled and deveined

1 tablespoon olive oil

1 tablespoon butter

½ cup diced fresh chives, plus 2 tablespoons for garnish

3 cloves fresh garlic, finely chopped

Juice and zest of 1 lemon

½ teaspoon ground paprika

Salt and pepper to taste

2 cups heavy cream

¾ cup shredded parmesan cheese

> **PAIR WITH:**
>
> • *Chocolate Peanut Butter Tart (page 165)*

Cook the pasta according to package instructions for al dente results. Sauté the shrimp in olive oil and butter in a large skillet until they just begin to curl, then add the chives, garlic, lemon juice and zest, paprika, salt, and pepper. Cook 2 to 3 minutes. Add the pasta and cream. Cook another 2 to 3 minutes, until the cream begins to thicken. Add the cheese and stir to incorporate. Sprinkle with the remaining chives, and serve with warm garlic knots.

Garlic Knots

Prep time: 15 minutes • Bake time: 15–20 minutes • Yield: 4 servings

16 ounces prepared, store bought (or homemade) pizza dough

2 tablespoons olive oil, divided

1 teaspoon sea salt

2 tablespoons butter

2 cloves fresh garlic, finely chopped

Salt and pepper to taste

1 tablespoon chopped parsley

Preheat oven to 375°. Cut the pizza dough in half evenly, then cut each half in half. Do this equally until you have 16 portions of dough. Roll each piece of dough between your hands into a 4- to 5-inch tube. Tie the dough into a single knot and place on a parchment paper-lined baking sheet. Continue to knot all 16 pieces of dough. Drizzle 1 tablespoon of olive oil over the knots, coating each one evenly. Sprinkle each knot lightly with sea salt. Bake 15 to 20 minutes, until lightly golden.

Heat the remaining olive oil and butter over medium heat in a small saucepan. Add the garlic, salt, pepper, and parsley. Cook mixture gently until it foams and sizzles, roughly 2 to 3 minutes, then set aside. Do not brown the garlic; adjust heat lower if needed.

Once the knots finish baking, quickly transfer them to a serving bowl, cover in the garlic butter, and toss to coat. Serve warm.

Eggplant Parmesan, Frisée Salad, and Cheesy Breadsticks

Eggplant Parmesan

Prep time: 45 minutes • Cook time: 30 minutes • Bake time: 35 minutes
Yield: 6 servings

2 medium-sized eggplants

Kosher salt

1 yellow onion, diced

½ cup butter

2 tablespoons olive oil

2 (27-ounce) cans crushed
tomatoes

2 cloves fresh garlic

Salt and pepper to taste

2 cups all-purpose flour

4 eggs

2 cups seasoned Italian bread
crumbs

2–3 cups light olive oil

3 cups shredded mozzarella
cheese

2 cups shredded parmesan
cheese

> **PAIR WITH:**
>
> * *Apple Cranberry Shortbread Crumble (page 172)*
>
> * *Wild Dried Blueberry Pound Cake (page 167)*

Slice each eggplant into one-inch slices and lightly sprinkle with salt. Set slices on a baking sheet lined with paper towels. Fill the baking sheet, then top the salted eggplant with another layer of paper towels and repeat for all the eggplant slices. Set aside.

Sauté the onions in butter and olive oil until tender. Add the tomatoes, garlic, salt, and pepper. Simmer uncovered 20 to 30 minutes while you fry the eggplant.

Preheat over to 350°. Set up 3 bowls: one with the flour, one with the beaten eggs, and the final with the bread crumbs. Remove the eggplant from the paper towels and dredge in flour, then in the beaten egg, and finally in the bread crumbs. Heat the olive oil in a 12-inch skillet over medium heat. Fry the eggplant 2 to 3 minutes per side, then set aside on a paper-towel-lined plate. Repeat this process until all the eggplant slices are breaded and fried.

Ladle 1 to 2 cups sauce into the bottom of a 9-by-13-inch glass baking dish. Add a layer of fried eggplant to the dish. Ladle 2 to 3 cups sauce over the top of the eggplant and sprinkle with one-third of the mozzarella and parmesan cheeses. Repeat this process until you've used all the eggplant and sauce, roughly three layers. Bake 35 minutes, uncovered. This provides a crispy, caramelized cheese layer. If you prefer a softer top, bake covered tightly in foil.

» Recipe continues on next page

» Continued

Frisée Salad

Prep time: 5 minutes • Yield: 4–6 servings

2 medium-sized heads frisée
   lettuce

1 medium-sized cucumber, sliced

2 tablespoons olive oil

2 tablespoons balsamic vinegar

1 tablespoon lemon juice

Salt and pepper to taste

Chop frisée into bite-sized pieces and add to a large salad bowl along with cucumber slices. Whisk remaining ingredients together in a separate bowl. Dress the salad when it's time to serve.

Cheesy Breadsticks

Prep time: 5 minutes • Cook time: 15 minutes • Yield: 4–6 servings

2 (12-ounce) boxes of crunchy
   breadsticks

½ cup butter

½ cup shredded parmesan cheese

1 teaspoon dried oregano

1 clove fresh garlic, smashed and
   finely chopped

Salt and pepper to taste

Preheat the oven to 350°. Line a rimmed baking sheet with parchment paper, and spread the breadsticks on it. Melt butter and add cheese and seasonings. Pour the cheesy butter over the breadsticks, covering evenly. Bake 15 minutes. Serve warm alongside the salad and eggplant parmesan.

For Fun + Littles

Cooking with kids in the kitchen is my greatest joy.

I read a barn wood sign once that said: "The most important work you'll ever do is within your home." That resonated with me. I have two precious boys who came earth side after wildly tough pregnancies, and when I think about all I do, I realize I'm solely motivated by providing a good life for my kids. I think any loving mother can agree she just wants the best for her children. We mess up and yell too much and fall short daily, but man, I love these little dudes fiercely. I am raising men here—I am now an expert in bodily functions, skinned knees, and temper tantrums—and these kiddos know how to treat a lady right. Plenty of snuggles, stinky tennis shoes, and kid clutter abound in the Kartes house.

Parenting is about growing up and learning the true meaning of life, all while trying to get your kids to eat something green, appreciate the value of a dollar, and become good grown-ups. I think about that sign all the time. I get busy, the house gets trashed, and I'm pretty sure my poor kids think clean laundry lives in the hallway outside the laundry room, where I toss dried clothes and then start another load. Sometimes, I shoulder heaps of guilt about how I'm parenting, feeling like it's not good enough, that I could do more, I could do better, and then, as soon as I open the dryer door and throw clean clothes out into the hall, my boys nosedive into the laundry, burying themselves in warm, fresh clothes, Noah squealing, "I hope it's towels. That covers you more!" Then I feel this sort of grace.

These kids have it good. We love them, they are making memories and doing kid stuff, and it's chaotic and fun. Noah is eight now, and the kid knows his way around a kitchen. He scrambles great eggs and is starting to feel proud of his culinary creations. Sometimes, when I drop him off at school and he runs away from the car with his too-big backpack flopping around off his shoulders, I'll roll the window down and yell, "What's for dinner?" He will always yell back, "Mac 'n' cheese! No veggies!" I'll laugh and yell after him, "Yes veggies!" He doesn't look back. Tears fill my eyes because I want to stop time and park the car and run after him and squish his cheeks and tell him this love I have for him ruins me in the best way. But I don't. I simply take a mental picture of him running from the car to meet his friends and be a kid.

Thinking back on their lives up to now, I have images in my mind that play in stop-motion, flashes, little mental movies of these kids growing up. First steps and delighted eyes at the zoo, crocodile tears because of smashed fingers, and granola bar chunks stuck in their hair. Road trip sing-alongs and candy-colored art projects aplenty. Eating corn dogs with delight, them saying, "No, no, Mama," to a bite of salad. I could keep going...

Raising children is sanctifying work. It's important. And you, my dear mama, are doing better than okay. You are doing the best job. They love you; you are their whole world. Embrace it. Don't wish away the hard years, for they are also the tender years.

Cooking with kids in the kitchen is my greatest joy. I'm already prone to messiness myself, so spilled flour and sticky hands faze me not. It drives Mike crazy when I get Milo out of his high chair after dinner and cut him loose, covered in the remnants of a mostly splattered meal! I'm like, "Whatever, no biggie," as Mike runs after him with a damp rag. Cook with your ragamuffins. Make eating fun and not a chore. I grew up on fish sticks and hamburger patties, so say goodbye to mom guilt over gourmet or exotic foods. Keep introducing vegetables to your littles. I read somewhere that it takes fifteen tries before we decide once and for all if we like a certain food, so keep on offering.

The meals in this section are fun and/or kid approved, and my munchkins gobble them up! My eight-year-old is my biggest critic, and he's been known to request *each* dish. So have a little fun! You can even prepare this kid-approved food for very grown-up dinner parties because, hey, I know there's a little munchkin in each one of us desperately wishing we were at the kid table when the adult table conversation gets a little dry.

Sticky, Spicy Oven-Baked Baby Back Ribs with Sesame Broccoli and Rice

Baby Back Ribs

Prep time: 10 minutes • Cook time: 2½ hours • Yield: 3–4 people

1 rack of baby back ribs, roughly 3 pounds

2 tablespoons brown sugar

2 tablespoons tamari or soy sauce

1 teaspoon ground black pepper

1 teaspoon garlic powder

2 tablespoons yellow or Dijon mustard

½ teaspoon kosher salt

½ teaspoon ground paprika

½ cup of your favorite hoisin/garlic Asian-style marinade

GARNISHES

1 cup sliced cashews

1 cup sliced radishes

1 cup thinly sliced green onions

1 bunch cilantro, chopped

2 limes, sliced

½ cup toasted, unsweetened coconut

> **PAIR WITH:**
> - *Wild Dried Blueberry Pound Cake (page 167)*
> - *Caramelized Banana Cream Pudding (page 180)*

Preheat grill to 250°. Lay a large sheet of heavy-duty foil on the grill, long enough to hold the ribs and their juices. Rub ribs with brown sugar, tamari, black pepper, garlic powder, mustard, salt, and paprika. Lay seasoned ribs on the grill and grill on low for 30 minutes. This step is purely for flavor and looks. The grill smoke will lacquer the meat. Preheat oven to 350°. Remove the meat from the grill, along with the foil (to reserve juices), and top with Asian-style marinade. Once the additional sauce is added, wrap the meat in existing foil tightly, place on a baking sheet, and bake 60 to 90 minutes. Ribs should be fall-apart tender and juicy. Allow to cool inside the foil 10 to 15 minutes before garnishing and slicing.

Sesame Broccoli

Cook time: 10 minutes • Yield: 4–6 servings

4–5 cups broccoli florets

Juice of 1 lime

1 clove fresh garlic, smashed

2 tablespoons sesame seeds

1 teaspoon toasted sesame oil

2 tablespoons olive oil

1 teaspoon brown sugar

Salt and pepper to taste

Bring two inches of water to a boil in a large pot with a lid. Add broccoli florets, steam 6 minutes, and drain. Add remaining ingredients to the same pot over medium heat. Add broccoli back to the sauce and stir to coat. Check for seasoning and add salt and pepper as needed. Serve with rice.

Recipe continues on next page

Grilled Lamb Kabobs and Red Quinoa and Tomato Grain Salad

Lamb Kabobs

Prep time: 20 minutes • Cook time: 15 minutes • Yield: 4–6 servings

> **PAIR WITH:**
> - *Homemade Limoncello (page 187)*
> - *Lime Tres Leches Cake (page 141)*

2 pounds lamb leg meat, cut into 2-inch squares

2 red bell peppers, cut into 2-inch pieces

2 yellow bell peppers, cut into 2-inch pieces

1 red onion, cut into 2-inch pieces

3 tablespoons olive oil

3 tablespoons fresh oregano, finely chopped

3 cloves fresh garlic, finely chopped

Juice and zest of 1 lemon

2 teaspoons kosher salt

1 teaspoon cracked black pepper

Place the lamb and vegetables in a large mixing bowl. Add the rest of the ingredients to the bowl, and mix thoroughly to coat the vegetables and meat. Marinate at room temperature for at least 30 minutes or up to 3 hours in the refrigerator. Soak bamboo skewers according to the package directions, and start the kabobs off with a piece of onion, then pepper, then meat. Repeat this process until you've filled your skewer. Repeat this process over again until you've used all your ingredients. Preheat your grill to 450°. Place the skewers on the hot grill, and cook for about 5 to 6 minutes on each side. This will give you a solid medium rare. Continue to cook until you've reached a temperature you are happy with.

Red Quinoa and Tomato Grain Salad

Prep time: 15 minutes • Yield: 4–6 servings

2 cups cooked red quinoa (any cooked grain can easily be substituted)

1 cup cherry tomatoes, halved

1 cup small mozzarella balls, halved

½ cup chopped walnuts

½ cup sliced radishes

¼ cup chopped fresh basil

¼ cup chopped fresh flat leaf parsley

CITRONETTE

½ cup olive oil

1 clove fresh garlic, finely crushed

Juice and zest of 1 lemon

Salt and pepper to taste

1 pinch crushed red pepper flakes

Add the grains, tomatoes, mozzarella, walnuts, radishes, and herbs to a mixing bowl. Whisk together the citronette ingredients in a separate bowl, then pour over the grains and gently mix. After about 20 minutes, you may need to add a touch more salt and pepper. Quinoa loves to soak up the flavor. This is best served at room temperature.

Sheet Pan Chicken Nachos, Fresh Guacamole, and Chili-Lime Pineapple Spears

Sheet Pan Chicken Nachos

Prep time: 15 minutes • Bake time: 8–10 minutes • Yield: 4–6 servings

1 (15-ounce) bag of your favorite taco chips

2 tablespoons olive oil

½ medium yellow onion, chopped

2 cloves fresh garlic, chopped

1 teaspoon garlic powder

1 teaspoon onion powder

1 teaspoon ground paprika

1 teaspoon taco seasoning

1 teaspoon ground turmeric

½ teaspoon kosher salt

3 cups shredded rotisserie chicken

4 ounces salsa

3 cups shredded cheddar cheese

1 (15-ounce) can pinto beans, drained

1 (15-ounce) can black olives, drained

1 cup cherry tomatoes, halved

1 bunch cilantro, chopped

1 bunch green onions, chopped

½ cup sour cream

1 jalapeño, sliced

> **PAIR WITH:**
>
> * *Irish Cream Mason Jars To Go (page 193), served alongside dessert*
>
> * *Olive Oil and Espresso Dark Chocolate Cake with Cream Cheese Buttercream and Caramel (page 171)*

Preheat oven to 350°. Lay the chips on a parchment-lined baking sheet. Sauté the onions, garlic, and spices in a large skillet in olive oil 2 to 3 minutes, until the onions are slightly tender and spices are toasted. Add the chicken meat and salsa to skillet. Toss to coat chicken in the seasonings and cook 3 to 4 minutes. Cover chips with the seasoned chicken, cheese, beans, olives, and tomatoes. Bake 8 to 10 minutes, or until the cheese is melted and bubbling. To finish the nachos, top with fresh cilantro, green onions, sour cream, and jalapeños!

Fresh Guacamole

Prep time: 10 minutes • Yield: 4–6 servings

4–6 ripe avocados

Juice of 1 lemon

Juice of 1 lime

1 cup chopped cilantro

2 tablespoons grated onion

1 teaspoon garlic powder

1 finely diced jalapeño (optional)

Salt and pepper to taste

Smash all ingredients together in a large bowl until you have a chunky guacamole. A potato masher works great for this. The lemon juice prevents browning, so don't skip it and just use lime juice. Serve with chips.

» Recipe continues on next page

Continued

Chili-Lime Pineapple Spears

Yield: 4–6 servings

1 large pineapple

Juice of 2 limes

1 tablespoon chili powder

Sea salt to taste

Remove the skin of the pineapple with a large knife, slicing 4 sides off the core. Discard the core. Slice each side into long strips. You should be able to get 4 to 6 spears out of each side of the pineapple. Squeeze fresh lime juice over the pineapple spears. Sprinkle with chili powder and sea salt.

Classic Baked Shells and Cheese with Oven-Roasted Lemon-Pepper Asparagus

Prep time: 15 minutes • Bake time: 20 minutes • Yield: 6–8 servings

BUTTERED BREAD CRUMB TOPPING

2 cups torn, stale bread of your choice

¼ cup chopped flat leaf parsley

¼ cup shredded parmesan cheese

2 tablespoons butter

Salt and pepper to taste

CLASSIC BAKED SHELLS AND CHEESE

12 ounces large-sized shell pasta (roughly ¾ of a standard one-pound box)

½ cup butter

2 tablespoons olive oil

1 clove fresh garlic, chopped

½ teaspoon ground paprika

Salt and pepper to taste

¼ cup all-purpose flour

½ teaspoon Dijon mustard

5 cups whole milk

3 cups shredded cheddar cheese

2 cups shredded parmesan cheese

> **PAIR WITH:**
>
> • *Short-Crust Sour Cherry Cobbler (page 148)*

Prepare the buttered bread crumb topping first. Pulse all the ingredients in a food processor until you've thoroughly mixed the bread crumbs but they still have some texture. The pulse setting works best for this. Set aside.

Preheat the oven to 400°. Cook the pasta al dente, according to the package instructions, in salted water. Make the cheese sauce while the noodles cook. Melt the butter and olive oil in a large nonstick pot, then sauté the garlic, paprika, and salt and pepper 1 to 2 minutes over medium heat. Add the flour and Dijon mustard. Stir to create a paste, and cook 2 to 3 minutes. Add the milk, and stir constantly until it thickens, roughly 5 to 7 minutes. Remove from heat and add cheese. Stir to melt, and taste for salt and pepper. Add the noodles and mix. Pour into a buttered 9-by-13-inch glass baking dish and top with buttered bread crumbs. Bake for up to 20 minutes.

Oven-Roasted Lemon-Pepper Asparagus

Prep time: 5 minutes • Cook time: 15 minutes • Yield: 4 servings

2 pounds trimmed asparagus

2 tablespoons olive oil

2 cloves fresh garlic, crushed and chopped

1 teaspoon cracked black pepper

Salt to taste

Zest of 1 lemon

Preheat oven to 400°. Combine asparagus, oil, garlic, pepper, and salt on a baking sheet, mixing to coat each piece. Roast for 15 minutes. Toss with the fresh lemon zest and serve.

Garlic and Anchovy Spaghetti with Bread Crumbs and Apple Cider Brussels Sprouts

Garlic and Anchovy Spaghetti

Prep time: 15 minutes • Cook time: 15 minutes • Yield: 2–4 servings

8–10 ounces dry spaghetti
noodles

6–8 anchovy fillets packed in
olive oil

¼ cup olive oil

6 cloves fresh garlic, crushed and
chopped

1 teaspoon cracked black pepper

¼ teaspoon crushed red pepper
flakes or 1 red Fresno chili,
sliced

Zest and juice of 1 lemon

1 cup reserved pasta cooking
water

Salt and pepper to taste

1 cup shredded parmesan cheese

PAIR WITH:

- *Pear Brandy (page 195), served alongside dessert*

- *One-Pan Lava Cake (page 175)*

Cook the pasta according to package instructions in salted water, and reserve one cup of pasta cooking water. Set the noodles aside. Melt anchovies in olive oil over medium heat in a large skillet with tall sides. Add the garlic, cracked black pepper, red pepper flakes or chili, and lemon zest and juice. Sauté one minute, until the garlic becomes fragrant. Add the cooked pasta and cooking water. Toss to coat the pasta, and season with the salt and pepper. Add the parmesan cheese and a generous amount of bread crumbs, just before serving, to keep them crisp.

Bread Crumbs

Prep time: 5 minutes • Cook Time: 3–4 minutes • Yield: 2–4 servings

2 cups torn stale bread of your
choice

¼ cup chopped flat leaf parsley

¼ cup shredded parmesan cheese

2 tablespoons butter

Salt and pepper to taste

Pulse all the ingredients in a food processor until you've thoroughly mixed the bread crumbs but they still have some texture. The pulse setting works nicely for this. Heat a skillet over medium to medium-high heat and sauté bread crumbs 3 to 4 minutes until fragrant and toasted. Toss with spaghetti.

Recipe continues on next page

Continued

Apple Cider Brussels Sprouts

Prep Time: 5 minutes • Cook time: 15 minutes • Yield: 2–4 servings

1 pound brussels sprouts, cleaned and trimmed

½ cup apple cider

2 tablespoons white vinegar

2 tablespoons olive oil

¼ teaspoon crushed red pepper flakes

Salt and pepper to taste

½ cup walnuts

1 clove fresh garlic, smashed and chopped

½ cup shaved parmesan cheese

Slice the brussels sprouts in half and place in a large soup pot with lid. Add apple cider and vinegar, and steam over medium-high heat for 3 to 4 minutes, until the liquid has completely evaporated. Add the olive oil, pepper flakes, and salt and pepper. Sauté until the sprouts begin to caramelize. Add the walnuts and garlic, and cook until fragrant. These last two steps happen quickly, so be mindful of not burning the walnuts and garlic. Top with shaved parmesan cheese.

The Last Meatball Recipe You'll Ever Need, Creamy Orzo, and Spinach and Basil Pesto

Meatballs

Prep time: 5 minutes • Cook time: 10–15 minutes
Yield: roughly 2 dozen meatballs

1 pound ground beef

1 pound ground breakfast
   sausage, or sausage of choice

⅓ cup finely crushed cracker
   crumbs

1 egg

1 teaspoon onion powder

1 teaspoon kosher salt

½ teaspoon cracked black pepper

½ teaspoon garlic powder

1 clove fresh garlic, finely minced

2 tablespoons olive oil for frying
   the meatballs

1–2 cups chicken stock, as
   needed

> **PAIR WITH:**
>
> * *Mulled Wine (page 205), serve chilled, skip the cinnamon*
>
> * *Double Peanut Marshmallow Treats (page 150), skip the peanuts and add one cup of chocolate chips*

> **TIPS:**
>
> * *Don't squeeze meatballs or roll them for too long. Meat mixture should retain the fat.*
>
> * *Use sausage for extra flavor. Ground pork is fine, just bump up your salt and seasonings.*
>
> * *Feel free to add ANYTHING to tailor these meatballs to your liking: ricotta, fresh parmesan, Dijon mustard, fresh herbs, or white wine. These are all excellent additions. This will be your holy grail meatball recipe to work from!*

Mix all the ingredients except the olive oil and the chicken stock, using two forks or your hand shaped into a stiff claw. Mix well, but do not squeeze the meat through your fingers or overmix. Mixture should appear aerated. Form the meatballs gently by hand or by using a self-release ice cream scoop, keeping the size to just under 1 ounce.

Heat the oil in a large nonstick skillet or cast iron over medium heat. Once the pan is hot, begin adding the meatballs. Fry 10 to 12 at a time. Rotate the meatballs every 2 minutes to evenly brown on all sides. While the meatballs cook, add the chicken stock and turn heat up to medium-high. Gently shake the pan to keep meatballs moving. Meatballs are ready once chicken stock has evaporated. The liquid will be gone and meat will be glossy and cooked through.

Recipe continues on next page

Continued

Creamy Orzo

Prep time: 15 minutes • Yield: 4–6 servings

1 (16-ounce) box orzo pasta	2 tablespoons butter	Zest of 1 lemon
2 cups heavy cream	½ teaspoon ground black pepper	
1 cup shredded parmesan cheese	Salt to taste	

Cook the orzo pasta al dente, according to package instructions. Drain the pasta thoroughly and return to pan over medium heat. Add the remaining ingredients and stir. Allow to cook 2 to 3 minutes, until the cheese is melted. Top with the meatballs and the spinach and basil pesto.

Spinach and Basil Pesto

(Nut free) • Yield: just over 1 cup

3 cups baby spinach	½ cup grated parmesan cheese	Juice and zest of 1 lemon
1 cup fresh, sweet basil leaves	1 clove fresh garlic	
¾ cup olive oil	Salt and pepper to taste	

Whirl all the ingredients in a food processor. Using the pulse option yields a pesto that retains some texture and won't be overly smooth. Refrigerate and use within 3 days.

Ranch Smash Burgers, Garlicky Green Beans, and Potato Wedges with Sour Cream Dressing

Ranch Dressing

Prep Time: 5 minutes • Inactive Time: 30 minutes • Yield: roughly 2 cups

1 cup mayonnaise

½ cup sour cream

¼ cup milk

1 tablespoon finely chopped fresh
   parsley

1 teaspoon dried rosemary

1 teaspoon fresh chives

1 teaspoon garlic powder

1 teaspoon onion powder

Salt and pepper to taste

> **PAIR WITH:**
>
> - *Beer and Grapefruit Spritzers (page 197)*
>
> - *Basic Not-Basic Chocolate Cream Pie (page 161)*

Mix all the ranch dressing ingredients thoroughly and allow to sit in the fridge for at least 30 minutes. Add more milk if you prefer a thinner dressing or dip.

Burgers

Prep time: 10 minutes • Cook time: 15–20 minutes • Yield: 8 burgers

2 pounds 85/15 ground beef

Salt and pepper to taste

8 slices Havarti cheese

1 cup prepared ranch dressing

1 cup spicy pickles

2 cups leafy baby greens

8 brioche buns

Divide the meat into eight portions. Heat a 12-inch skillet or grill over medium heat. Smash burgers into thin rounds larger than the width of your bun, as meat will shrink during cooking. Season with salt and pepper. Cook the beef patties 3 to 4 minutes per side, until cooked to your preferred wellness. During the last minute of cooking, add the Havarti. Top with the ranch dressing, spicy pickles, and greens on top of your brioche bun.

Recipe continues on next page

Ranch Smash Burgers, Garlicky Green Beans, and Potato Wedges with Sour Cream Dressing

86

Continued

Garlicky Green Beans

Prep time: 10 minutes • Yield: 4–6 servings

1½ pounds green beans, trimmed

2 tablespoon olive oil

2 cloves fresh garlic, smashed
and chopped

Salt and pepper to taste

Sauté green beans in olive oil 2 to 3 minutes over medium-high heat. Add ¼ cup water and cook with the lid on for another 2 to 3 minutes, until the water has evaporated. Remove the lid and add the garlic and salt and pepper. You may need to remove the lid and sauté a minute or two longer in order to evaporate remaining water.

Potato Wedges

Prep Time: 10 minutes • Cook Time: 35–45 minutes • Yield: 4–6 servings

8 medium-sized Yukon gold
potatoes

¼ cup olive oil

Salt and pepper to taste

Preheat the oven to 375°. Slice each potato in half, then in half again. Continue until you have eight wedges per potato. Toss the potatoes in oil, salt, and pepper on a rimmed baking sheet. Bake 35 to 45 minutes, or until the potatoes are golden and tender.

Buttermilk Grilled Chicken, Parmesan Ditalini and Peas, and Buttery Dinner Rolls

Buttermilk Grilled Chicken

Prep time: 5 minutes plus overnight marinade • Cook time: 20 minutes
Yield: 4–6 servings

4–6 large chicken breasts

2 tablespoons olive oil

2 cups buttermilk

2 teaspoons garlic powder

2 teaspoons kosher salt

2 teaspoons onion powder

1 teaspoon cracked black pepper

PAIR WITH:

- *Apricot and Chocolate Rolls (page 151)*

Place the chicken in a gallon-sized freezer bag. Add the buttermilk and seasonings. Remove as much air from the bag as possible and swish it around a bit to mix. Place on a plate and on the lowest shelf in your refrigerator. Marinate overnight. Remove the chicken from the refrigerator at least one hour before grilling. Preheat grill to 350°. Place chicken on the grill and rotate every 3 to 4 minutes. Be careful to avoid flare-ups and close the lid. It should take about 20 minutes to cook the chicken to 165°.

Parmesan Ditalini and Peas

Prep time: 5 minutes • Cook time: 15 minutes • Yield: 4–6 servings

1 (16-ounce) box ditalini short pasta

1 (12-to-16-ounce) bag petite frozen peas or 2 cups fresh hulled peas

2 cups heavy cream

1 tablespoon butter

1 teaspoon onion powder

½ teaspoon cracked black pepper

1 cup shredded parmesan cheese

Kosher salt to taste

Cook pasta according to package instructions, drain, then add the pasta back to the pot. Add peas, cream, butter, onion powder, and pepper, and cook over medium-low heat. Cream will begin to thicken after about 2 minutes. Add cheese and season with salt, then stir to melt.

Recipe continues on next page

Continued

Buttery Dinner Rolls

Prep time: 10 minutes • Inactive time: 2 hours • Cook time: 30–40 minutes
Yield: 12 large rolls

2 teaspoons quick yeast

1 cup warm milk

3 cups all-purpose flour

2 tablespoons butter, softened

2 tablespoons sugar

1 teaspoon kosher salt

1 egg

* *If the dough is too wet, add the flour 1 tablespoon at a time. If too dry, add the warm milk 1 tablespoon at a time.*

** *At this point, if you have a bread machine, place dough inside and choose the dough setting.*

Add the yeast to warm milk and allow it to bloom about 5 minutes, until foamy. Add to the bowl of a stand mixer along with the remaining dough ingredients* and mix using the dough hook, 6 to 7 minutes. This can also be done by hand. Allow the dough to rest 2 to 3 minutes and knead again 6 to 7 minutes**. Cover with a damp kitchen towel and allow to rise 45 minutes in a warm place or proofing drawer. Once the dough is finished with its first rise, preheat oven to 350°. Generously butter a 9-by-13-inch pan. Turn the dough out onto a lightly floured surface. Divide the dough in half, then divide those halves in half. Continue until you have 12 equal portions. Shape the dough into balls and place them in the 9-by-13-inch pan. Allow to rise 20 to 30 minutes. Drizzle the melted butter over top of the rolls before baking. Bake 30 to 40 minutes, or until the rolls are lightly browned and cooked through.

Barbecue Chicken Legs, Zucchini and Fresh Corn Fritters with Sun-Dried Tomato Aioli, and Creamy Traditional Coleslaw

Barbecue Chicken Legs

Prep time: 15 minutes • Bake time: 60–90 minutes • Yield: 4–6 servings

PAIR WITH:
- *Peachy Basil Lemonade (page 213)*

18–20 chicken legs

Salt and pepper to taste

1 cup ketchup

¼ cup mustard

¼ cup soy sauce

2 tablespoons brown sugar

2 cloves fresh garlic, chopped

1 tablespoon olive oil

1 tablespoon Worcestershire sauce

½ teaspoon cracked black pepper

Splash of hot sauce

Preheat oven to 350°. Lay the chicken legs in the bottom of a baking dish with a lid. Dutch ovens or casserole pans work great for this. Season the chicken legs with salt and pepper. Whisk together the remaining ingredients in a separate bowl to make the barbecue sauce. Pour the sauce over legs and toss to coat evenly. This step can be done up to one day in advance, and the dressed chicken can be refrigerated in a freezer bag. Bake the chicken legs 60 to 90 minutes.

Zucchini and Fresh Corn Fritters

Cook time: 20 minutes • Yield: roughly 12 fritters

2 small to medium zucchinis, grated, roughly 3 cups

1/2 teaspoon kosher salt

2 ears of corn, kernels sliced off cob

1 egg

1 cup whole milk

1 cup all-purpose flour

1 teaspoon baking powder

1 cup grated parmesan cheese

1 teaspoon onion powder

1 teaspoon garlic powder

Salt and pepper to taste

1 cup olive oil for shallow fry

Sea salt for finishing

Place zucchini and kosher salt in a bowl, stir, and let stand 10 minutes. Squeeze and discard as much liquid as possible from zucchini by pressing it firmly against the side of the bowl with a hand, dumping liquid into the sink. Mix all ingredients except olive oil and sea salt in a large mixing bowl. Heat olive oil in a 12-inch skillet over medium heat. Scoop several piles of fritter batter into the pan using a one-ounce self-release ice cream scooper. Use a fork to flatten them out slightly for even cooking. Cook 2 to 3 minutes per side until golden and cooked through. Repeat this process using all the batter. Sprinkle cooked fritters with a little sea salt to finish.

» Recipe continues on next page

– Continued

Sun-Dried Tomato Aioli

Prep time: 5 minutes • Yield: roughly 1 1/2 cups

1 cup mayonnaise

1/2 cup diced sun-dried tomatoes in oil

1 tablespoon lemon juice

1/2 cup grated parmesan cheese

Salt and pepper to taste

Mix all ingredients well. Chill and serve. Keeps well in the refrigerator up to 4 days.

Creamy Traditional Coleslaw

Prep time: 10 minutes • Yield: 4–6 servings

1 cup mayonnaise

2 tablespoons granulated sugar

½ cup white vinegar

½ teaspoon ground black pepper

½ teaspoon celery seeds

½ teaspoon garlic powder

½ teaspoon kosher salt

4–6 cups shredded cabbage

2 stalks celery, thinly sliced

Whisk the dressing ingredients in a large enough bowl to hold the cabbage and celery. Add cabbage and celery and mix thoroughly. Allow coleslaw to sit about 30 minutes or up to three hours in the fridge before serving.

Focaccia MLTs (Mozzarella, Lettuce, and Tomato) with Sweet Potato Fries

This focaccia sandwich is heavily inspired by one of my cooking heroes, Alexandra Stafford (@ alexandracooks on Instagram). She introduced me to this dreamy focaccia bread that has now become a staple in my home. When I was in the hospital with Milo, she sent me the sweetest package with her brilliant book, *Bread Toast Crumbs*, complete with Pyrex bowls and bowl covers. Her kindness meant the world to me, and I'm mildly obsessed with her style of cooking. She has a gift, and these sandwiches are absolutely inspired by her magical, stunning focaccia sandwiches. Thank you, Alexandra, for being such a light and source of joy.

Focaccia

Prep time: 15 minutes • Inactive time: 2–3 hours • Bake time: 25–30 minutes
Yield: 4–6 servings

4 cups all-purpose flour

2 teaspoons active dry yeast

2 teaspoons kosher salt

½ cup olive oil, to be divided between the loaves

Sea salt for garnish

> **PAIR WITH:**
>
> * *Vanilla Panna Cotta and Citrus Caramel (page 147)*
>
> * *Chocolate Peanut Butter Tart (page 165)*

Mix the flour, yeast, and kosher salt with 2 cups warm water; do not knead. Cover with a towel and allow to sit on the counter four hours. You can also do this overnight in the refrigerator. Generously butter 2 9-inch pie plates or round pans. Add one tablespoons of olive oil to each pan. Divide the dough into two equal portions. Place one half into each prepared pan. Gently fold the dough into itself and flip over. Leave to rise on the counter 2 to 4 hours. Do not touch it. When ready to bake, preheat the oven to 425°. Pour two tablespoons of olive oil over top of focaccia loaves, and with an open hand, fingers bent, press gently and firmly into dough to create the signature valleys. Do this 4 to 5 times with each loaf. Be careful not to flatten the air pockets in the dough. Sprinkle with sea salt, and bake 25 minutes or until perfectly golden and crisp. Cook and slice in half lengthwise to make top and bottom slices.

» Recipe continues on next page

Continued

MLTs (Mozzarella, Lettuce, and Tomato)
Prep time: 5 minutes • Yield: 4–6 servings

Spinach Basil Pesto (page 84)
plus ½ cup mayonnaise

16 ounces fresh mozzarella
cheese (normally sold in
4-to-8-ounce balls)
3–4 cups baby spinach

3–4 large tomatoes, sliced
Salt and pepper to taste
1 pound or 16 slices cooked
bacon (optional)

Spread ¼ cup mayonnaise mix on the bottoms of both the bread rounds. Evenly distribute the ingredients between sandwiches. Place the tops on sandwiches and slice each round into 8 pieces. Serve with sweet potato fries.

Sweet Potato Fries
Prep time: 5 minutes • Cook time: 35–45 minutes • Yield: 4–6 servings

4–6 medium sized sweet
potatoes

¼ cup olive oil

Salt and pepper to taste

Preheat the oven to 375°. Slice each potato in half, then in half again. Continue this process until you have 8 wedges per potato. Toss the potatoes in olive oil, salt, and pepper on a rimmed baking sheet. Bake 35 to 45 minutes or until the potatoes are golden and tender. Pay close attention to the potatoes, as they have a high sugar content and can burn easily.

Creamy Tomato and Pumpkin Soup and Pan-Fried Cheese Sandwiches

Creamy Tomato and Pumpkin Soup

Prep time: 10 minutes • Cook time: 30 minutes • Yield: 4 servings

6 strips thick center-cut bacon, chopped

1½ cups pumpkin purée (canned is fine)

4 fresh tomatoes or 1 (15-ounce) can tomatoes

1 medium onion, chopped

1 red bell pepper, seeded and sliced

2 cloves fresh garlic

1 pinch crushed red pepper flakes

Salt and pepper to taste

4 cups chicken stock

½ cup heavy cream, for serving

1 cup chopped scallions, for serving

> **PAIR WITH:**
>
> • *Magic Shell and Pistachio Sundaes (page 162)*

Sauté the bacon in a large soup pot until crispy, then remove. Throw all the vegetables and seasonings into the bacon fat over medium heat, and sauté until soft. Add the chicken stock, and simmer 10 minutes. Whirl it all up with a stick blender or in your blender. Serve the soup with grilled cheese sandwiches, and top each bowl with crispy bacon, cream, and chopped scallions.

Pan-Fried Cheese Sandwiches

Cook time: 15–20 minutes • Yield: 8 sandwiches

3 cups shredded cheddar cheese

1 cup shredded parmesan cheese

1 16-ounce loaf country-style Italian bread, such as Pugliese, sliced into 16 slices

½ cup olive oil

Combine all the shredded cheese and set aside. Heat one tablespoon of olive oil in a large skillet over medium heat. Lay one bread slice in the pan, and top with 3 to 4 tablespoons shredded cheese. Place another bread slice on top, and fry 2 to 3 minutes, until the bottom slice is golden brown. Using a spatula, lift the sandwich out and pour another tablespoon of olive oil in the pan. Flip sandwich to place uncooked side down, and crisp 2 to 3 minutes, until golden brown. Continue this process until you've used all the bread, cheese, and oil. You will need less oil as you continue to make the sandwiches, due to residual oil in the pan. A half cup will be plenty for 8 sandwiches.

For Love

*Once we've been given what we're hungering for,
there is a period of calm and feeling loved.*

For me, food hasn't really ever been about how delicious something was. The more I think about food and what it means to my soul, it's always the emotion running alongside whatever I'm eating that stands out. We've been taught for so long that emotional eating is wrong, that it's a crutch. Attempting to feed our emotions will lead to indulgence, shame, unhealthiness, etc. Of course, some of these sentiments ring true. But what if we allowed ourselves the joy associated with food? When I am alone and eat something that's wonderful, I can't wait to share it. I want to revel in that moment of bliss and love by sharing the memory.

Food carries with it so many aspects we sometimes barely consider. I eat so many meals these days that are associated with powerful, lovely memories. Sometimes, a memory that is painful or bittersweet can tie itself to a particular meal because it's a reminder of a loved one who has passed on or moved away, but there is a certain beauty in this as well. You can, in a very tangible way, re-experience the past through food. Also, there is something simply splendid about satisfying hunger. When we are hungry for food or love or companionship or a break or grace, once we've been given what we are hungering for, there is a period of calm and feeling loved.

While I was in Boston on a solo work trip recently, I missed my husband desperately. I kept thinking, *I wish he could see this. I wish he could walk these streets and laugh with me*. I wanted him to see what I was seeing and feel what I was feeling. The value of alone time is not lost on me, and it's healthy and wonderful to be alone and lean into God. It's something I treasure. But on this one particular Boston evening, I went to a bar for my very first lobster-in-a-restaurant experience. I don't mean that miniscule lobster tail served beside an eight-ounce steak filet now. I've done that before, and it's fantastic. But I mean full-on, cold water, pulled from the North Atlantic just a stone's throw away eight hours ago *lobster*, intact, claws on, served straight-up, steamed, with a nutcracker and a vat of melted butter. In short, the stuff dreams are made of.

◆ ·

It went a little something like this: An excruciatingly long line of people waiting to be checked in by the hostess. A packed bar to the left and a packed house in the dining area to the right. I waited nearly an hour just to work my way up to the hostess stand. "Table for one!" I shouted. The music was loud, and the air smelled like a bar, naturally. The hostess leaned in and shouted back: "We don't seat parties of one! Head to the bar." I glanced over at this nightmarish option, then told her, "I want to order a lobster!" She said with finality, "Order it at the bar!" It was late, I was hungry, and things weren't looking good here. I beheld the crowd of drunken, happy people with beers in their hands. The bar was crazy busy. They didn't seat parties of one? Really? I pleaded. The bar looked like it was full of would-be lovers, battling for attention. I hadn't pushed my way into a meat market like this since my early twenties. It was chaos: loud music and wall-to-wall people sloshing drinks. Not one person in the bar was eating any food. "Surely, you can squeeze little, thirty-six-year-old me in the dining area, can't you?" She shook her head. In the bar, dude bros and lone wolves scanned the room, hoping to catch someone's eye. I tried to reason with this immoveable rock of a hostess: "C'mon, I'm too old for this. Lemme just get a lobster. It's my first time in Boston!" She leaned in and shouted over the noise, "It's the bar or nothin'. Sorry!" With her thick Boston accent, *sorry* came out *saaary*. I turned to leave, dejected, then stopped.

Nah, I was gonna do it. I burrowed my way through the mob to the bar. Folks waved credit cards, shouting drink orders at the bartenders. *Man*, I thought, *I do not miss this scene*. I wiggled my way up and, after determining that waiting patiently for my turn wasn't going to gain any traction here, I ended up aggressively taking my turn. "I want a lobster!" Shouting. "Here?" the girl behind the bar said. "Yup!" She said, "One, two, or three pound?" I said, "Three pounds." She looked surprised. "In my defense," I said, "most of the weight's in the shell, right?" She pointed at a barback: "Get that lady a stool!" She wiped my patch of the bar and squirted water into a plastic cup from a foot away.

I just sat there, waiting. *Why am I doing this?* There were so many people here, not on their phones, legitimately looking for a date, for love. After twenty minutes, my lobster came out. It was massive. There was a tiny side salad and this mammoth beast of a crustacean, piping hot and accompanied by a big ol' bowl of butter.

Thirty seconds before, I was invisible, but now I was on Front Street. Not a single other person in this bar was eating or even seated. I felt a twinge of loneliness. Man, here I was, and I just wanted my husband to be here with me. This sort of stuff was meant to share; this experience was the kind of thing we should be doing together. I wasn't supposed to be eating this alone. I hesitated a bit, then thought, *Okay, here goes, I'm enjoying this even if it's a rough setting*.

The bar area was getting more crowded by the moment. People were absolutely watching me at this point. Except the setting, this is basically my dream: just me and this lobster the size of my arm. No fork (I don't know why I didn't think to ask for one), I just dug in and started making quick work of the lobster. More and more people began staring. A guy came up and said, "You're a badass. No beer for me—gimme the lobster!" I felt like a hero of some sort. Two girls worked their way over, and one of them said, "You know, you're just tearing into that lobster right here, and now we want a lobster!" Now, instead of awkwardness, this thing was sort of a celebration, like *Oh yeah, you can totally do that!* This is a lobster

Are the wonderful experiences we have as wonderful if we aren't able to share them?

restaurant, right? I drew plenty of attention and was covered in butter. I finished my dinner, and an older woman slipped right into my seat as I stood up, her husband at her side. She said, "You've got the right idea. We saw you waiting from the restaurant side. We want the same thing you had!"

I closed my tab and worked my way back through the crowd, feeling a little proud. I walked to the back of the restaurant to wash up—wet naps can only take buttery hands so far. I really started thinking about this lobster and what he meant, philosophically. I eat alone in every city I work in, and I don't mind. It's become very normal for me. Sometimes, I prefer dinner by myself to gather my thoughts and clean house mentally. But this lobster was different. I'd just had this funny, strange experience, but I couldn't high-five anybody about it. I went back to my hotel room alone, and even with the time change, the kids were in bed back at home, so it was too late to even call Mike and tell him about it right afterward. I find myself longing to share every wild thing in this life with Mike. The one thought I had on repeat while tearing into that massive beast of a lobster was *I wish my darling friend were with me.*

This was when the concept for this book really came about. Are the wonderful experiences we have as wonderful if we aren't able to share them, to laugh about them afterward, and to relive them from time to time when a breeze brings the memory sailing back in? I want to share everything with Mike—everything that makes me laugh and cry, the things that make me whole, that tear my heart up. We have beautiful children together. He is my sweetest friend and my biggest champion. The experience of living, with all its ups and downs, with all its beautiful messiness, is something I want to share with this man, always.

And that's what the lobster that night in Boston taught me. I believe the value in food exists not only in the ingredients, the preparation, and the taste. There is another asset here to consider: the experiences that revolve around food. Specifically, shared experiences with that special someone. The food in this chapter is meant to be shared with somebody you love. It's food you can connect over, no tiny voices grumbling about it because it's too spicy or too exotic. These are just plain delicious dishes, perfect for celebrating the majesty of love, whether the relationship is new or half a century old.

Crispy Sweet Chili and Sesame Shrimp with Ginger Peanut Noodles

Crispy Sweet Chili and Sesame Shrimp with Ginger Peanut Noodles

Crispy Sweet Chili and Sesame Shrimp

Prep time: 10 minutes • Cook time: 10–12 minutes • Yield: 4 servings

PAIR WITH:

- *Virgin Mary Mix (page 201)*
- *Molten Chocolate and Caramel Cake (page 176)*

1 pound jumbo 14–16 count shrimp, peeled and deveined

1 teaspoon sesame oil

½ teaspoon garlic powder

½ teaspoon kosher salt

Cracked black pepper to taste

½ cup cornstarch

½ cup neutral oil suitable for frying

SAUCE

2 tablespoons butter

1 clove fresh garlic, chopped

1 red Fresno chili, sliced

¼–⅓ cup prepared sweet chili sauce

Squeeze of lime juice

Squeeze of mandarin orange juice

1 tablespoon white sesame seeds

½ cup chopped green onions

Add sesame oil, garlic powder, salt, and pepper to a large bowl, then add shrimp, tossing to coat. Place cornstarch in a separate bowl. Dip each shrimp into the cornstarch, then shake off excess vigorously. The cornstarch will taste chalky if there is too much on the shrimp. Heat the oil in a large skillet over medium-high heat until it shimmers but does not smoke. Add the cornstarch-dusted shrimp. Fry on each side until golden and crisp, roughly 1 to 2 minutes per side. Remove the cooked shrimp and place on a paper towel to remove excess oil.

Pour the remaining oil in the pan out into a mug for discarding, and return pan to stove. Melt the butter in the pan over medium-high heat, and add garlic and chili. Heat until garlic is fragrant, 1 to 2 minutes. Add the chili sauce and citrus juices. Heat the sauce until bubbling, 2 minutes. Place the shrimp into the hot sauce and stir to coat. Add the sesame seeds and green onions, then toss to coat. Serve with rice or plain for a fun appetizer.

Recipe continues on next page

Continued

Ginger Peanut Noodles

Prep time: 15 minutes • Yield: 4 servings

10 ounces dry spaghetti noodles

1 cup chopped toasted peanuts

½ cup chopped cilantro

½ cup chopped green onions

¼ cup olive oil

Juice of 2 limes

2 tablespoons soy sauce

2 tablespoons rice wine vinegar

2 tablespoons toasted sesame seeds

1 tablespoon grated fresh ginger

1 tablespoon sambal chili paste

(or less depending on desired spiciness)

1 teaspoon brown sugar

¼ cup pasta water, to thin the sauce

Cook the noodles according to package instructions, reserving one cup of the pasta cooking liquid. Drain the pasta. Whisk together remaining ingredients except pasta water in a large mixing bowl. Add cooked pasta to the bowl, and mix to coat noodles in sauce. Thin, if necessary, with pasta cooking water in 2-tablespoon increments. This pasta is excellent served hot or cold.

Fiery, Sweet Asian Salmon with Rice Noodles and Quick Pickled Cucumbers

Fiery, Sweet Asian Salmon

Cook time: 20–22 minutes • Yield: 4 servings

2 pounds of your favorite salmon
    fillet

¼ cup rice vinegar

2 tablespoons tamari or soy sauce

1 tablespoon gochujang (Sriracha
    works great if you can't find
    gochujang)

1 tablespoon sambal chili paste

1–2 teaspoons apricot jam or
    honey

1 teaspoon yellow mustard

1 clove fresh garlic, crushed

GARNISHES

1 cup chopped cilantro

1 cup chopped, dry roasted,
    salted peanuts

1 cup green onions, sliced

2–3 Fresno chilies, thinly sliced

2 tablespoons toasted sesame
    seeds

PAIR WITH:

- *Mom's Wine Punch (page 194)*
- *Creamy Lime Tart (page 159)*
- *Cream Coconut Cake (page 156)*

* *If the noodles are imported from Asia, they may not have directions, or the directions may be in an unfamiliar language. Lowering the noodles into boiling water in batches for 2 to 3 minutes yields a noodle with bite that doesn't fall apart. Immediately rinse the rice noodles in cool water to stop the cooking process. If you cannot find rice noodles, use angel hair pasta or spaghetti noodles in a pinch.*

Preheat your oven to 375°. Line a rimmed baking sheet with parchment paper. Rinse and pat dry the salmon fillet. Whisk the glaze ingredients into a thick sauce, and pour over the salmon, coating it completely. Bake 20 to 22 minutes for well-done salmon. Once the fish is baked, sprinkle half of all garnishes on top, reserving the other half for the noodles.

Recipe continues on next page

FOR LOVE

Fiery, Sweet Asian Salmon with Rice Noodles and Quick Pickled Cucumbers

108

» *Continued*

Quick Pickled Cucumbers

Prep Time: 5 minutes • Yield: 4 servings

½ cup rice vinegar

1 English cucumber, sliced into matchsticks

Salt and pepper to taste

To prepare the pickled cucumber, allow the cucumber to steep in the rice vinegar, and season with salt and pepper.

Rice Noodles

Prep Time: 5 minutes • Cook time: 10 minutes • Yield: 4 servings

16 ounces rice noodles like vermicelli

½ cup rice vinegar

½ cup tamari or soy sauce

2 tablespoons sweet chili sauce

1 tablespoon toasted sesame seeds

1 clove fresh garlic, crushed

1 teaspoon sambal chili paste

½ teaspoon ground black pepper

Whisk together the noodle sauce ingredients and set aside. The sauce tastes better the longer the ingredients mingle.

Cook the noodles according to the package instructions*. Rinse cooked noodles in cold water, and place in a bowl with the pickled cucumber. Chopped carrots and cabbage are also lovely options for pickling. Cover the noodles with the remaining garnishes and noodle sauce. Toss and serve with the salmon. Use any leftover sauce on the salmon as well, if desired.

Garlic and Lemon Cacio e Pepe with Roasted Artichokes and Aioli

Garlic and Lemon Cacio e Pepe

Prep time: 10 minutes • Cook time: 15 minutes • Yield: 4 servings

8–10 ounces uncooked thin
   spaghetti pasta
½ cup butter
1½ teaspoons cracked black
   pepper
1 tablespoon lemon zest
2 cloves fresh garlic, finely chopped

1 cup pasta water
1½ cups parmesan cheese plus
   an extra sprinkling for garnish
Kosher salt to taste
Squeeze of lemon juice

> **PAIR WITH:**
>
> • *Crème de Cassis (page 189), floated on champagne*
>
> • *One-Pan Lava Cake (page 175)*

Boil the pasta until it is almost al dente in a large pot of salted water. Melt the butter in a large skillet. Add the pepper, and sizzle it in the butter 1 to 2 minutes to bloom the spice. Add the lemon zest and chopped garlic. Sauté for another minute, then add the pasta water and cooked pasta. Toss to coat, and add the parmesan cheese. Continue gently tossing the pasta in the buttery sauce until cheese is melted. Add more pasta water as needed, and season with kosher salt. Serve with a squeeze of lemon juice and more parmesan cheese.

Roasted Artichokes and Aioli

Bake time: 35–45 minutes • Yield: 2–4 servings

1 cup mayonnaise
¼ cup grated parmesan cheese
Juice of 1 lemon

1 clove fresh garlic, finely
   chopped
½ teaspoon cracked black pepper

2 large artichokes
2 tablespoons olive oil
Kosher salt to taste

Preheat the oven to 375°. Mix the mayonnaise, parmesan cheese, lemon juice, garlic, and pepper in a bowl. Trim and wash the artichokes. Pour 1 tablespoon olive oil over each artichoke, and wrap individually in foil. Place on a rimmed baking sheet, and roast 35 to 45 minutes until very tender. Check tenderness by piercing with a knife at the base of the artichoke. Sprinkle a bit of kosher salt on artichokes, and serve alongside aioli for dipping. The aioli may be stored in the refrigerator up to 2 days.

Pan-Seared Dill and Caper Halibut, Black Pepper and Parmesan Risotto, and Garlicky Asparagus

Pan-Seared Dill and Caper Halibut

Cook time: 15 minutes • Yield: 2–4 servings

4 tablespoons butter

1 tablespoon olive oil

1½ pounds fresh halibut

Kosher salt and pepper to taste

1 (2-ounce) jar brined capers, drained

1 cup rosé wine

2 tablespoons chopped dill

PAIR WITH:

• *Strawberry Bellini (page 209)*

• *Creamy Lime Tart (page 159)*

* *Our fish was 2 inches thick. A thinner cut will cook and brown much faster.*

Heat 3 tablespoons butter and olive oil over medium-high heat in a large nonstick skillet until butter foams. Season the fish with kosher salt and pepper to taste. Lay the fish into hot fat skin-side down, and sear for 3 to 4 minutes*. Gently flip the fish, and add capers and wine. The fish will continue to poach for roughly 3 additional minutes. Do not overcook fish. Fish should be opaque with clear juices but very moist and tender. Remove the fish from the pan and reduce sauce by 1/3. Finish with last tablespoon of butter, and spoon sauce over fish to serve.

Black Pepper and Parmesan Risotto

Prep time: 10 minutes • Cook time: 30–35 minutes • Yield: 4 servings

2 tablespoons butter

1 tablespoon olive oil

½ cup chopped red onion or shallot

½ teaspoon cracked black pepper

1 cup arborio rice

1 cup rosé or white wine

4 cups chicken stock

½ cup heavy cream

½ cup grated parmesan cheese

Kosher salt to taste

Sauté the onion and black pepper in olive oil and butter over medium heat in a large heavy-bottomed saucepan until the onions are translucent, about 3 to 4 minutes. Add the rice, and toast in onions and oil 2 to 3 minutes. Add the wine, and stir continually until it has completely absorbed. Add 1 cup of stock at a time, and stir the rice continually until each addition of stock is completely absorbed. Once all the stock has been added and the rice is fully cooked and has a creamy texture, add the cream and cheese. Season with kosher salt to taste. Serve immediately.

» Recipe continues on next page

Continued

Garlicky Asparagus

Cook time: 10 minutes • Yield: 4 servings

2 pounds fresh asparagus, trimmed

Kosher salt to taste

2 tablespoons butter

2 cloves fresh garlic, finely chopped or smashed

Fresh cracked black pepper to taste

Steam trimmed asparagus seasoned with salt in 1 cup water in a large skillet over medium-high heat for roughly 3 minutes, then drain. Add butter, garlic, and pepper. Sauté 2 to 3 minutes and serve.

Lobster Dinner Splurge, Dreamy Dauphinoise Potatoes, and Mâché Caesar Salad

Lobster

Prep and cook time: 15 minutes • Yield: 2–4 servings

3 lobsters

1 cup butter

2 cloves fresh garlic, smashed

Sea salt to taste

PAIR WITH:

- *Caramelized Banana Cream Pudding (page 180)*

You can serve one lobster per guest, but I like to make 3 when it's just Mike and me, or you can prepare just the tails if you wish. I don't typically purchase the huge lobsters—the 1-pounders are sweet and delicious.

If lobsters have not been steamed, steam them in a large pot of shallow boiling water 8 minutes per pound, then set aside. Melt butter, garlic, and sea salt in a saucepan over medium heat. Allow lobsters to rest 10 to 15 minutes before serving. To remove tail, twist from the body. Use nutcrackers to break the claws and expose the meat, and cut the tail shell open with kitchen shears. Serve with a small dish of the garlic butter for dunking.

Dauphinoise Potatoes

Prep time: 10 minutes • Cook time: 45 minutes • Yield: 2–4 servings

8–10 small gold potatoes

2 tablespoons butter

2 cloves fresh garlic, chopped

2 sprigs lemon thyme or any

preferred fresh, woody herb

Kosher salt to taste

½ teaspoon cracked black pepper

1 tablespoon all-purpose flour

3 cups heavy cream

2 cups shredded parmesan cheese

Preheat oven to 350° and generously butter a 9-by-13-inch pan. Boil the potatoes in salted water 10 to 15 minutes. Drain and rinse in cool water. Slice potatoes as thinly as you can. Melt the butter, and add the garlic, herbs, salt, and pepper in a medium-sized saucepan. Cook until the butter begins to foam and garlic is fragrant, about two minutes. Add the flour, and stir to create a paste. Add the cream, and allow to thicken slightly. Place a layer or two of potatoes in the prepared pan, and add half the cream mixture. Sprinkle with 1 cup parmesan cheese. Add the remaining potatoes and cream on top. Sprinkle the remaining cheese over top of the potatoes. Bake 30 to 40 minutes.

Recipe continues on next page

Continued

Mâché Caesar Salad

Prep time: 10 minutes • Yield: 2–4 servings

OLIVE OIL CROUTONS

2–3 cups torn artisan bread

¼ cup olive oil

Sea salt to taste

CAESAR DRESSING

2 egg yolks

3–4 anchovy fillets, packed in oil

1 teaspoon cracked black
pepper

Juice of 2 small Meyer
lemons

1 teaspoon Dijon mustard

1 cup light olive oil

¾ cup finely grated parmesan
cheese

SALAD

4–6 cups mâché lettuce (spinach
and red leaf lettuce make a
great substitution)

1 cup shaved parmesan cheese

Sauté bread in olive oil until crisp and golden brown. Season with sea salt.

Blend all the ingredients except the oil and parmesan cheese in a food processor until creamy.
Slowly stream in the oil until dressing thickens. Be careful not to overmix. Fold in the parmesan.

Gently toss the lettuce with the dressing in a large bowl, and top with croutons and cheese.

Zesty Buffalo-Style Rack of Lamb with Crunchy Celery and Blue Cheese Salad

Prep time: 15 minutes • Cook time: 20 minutes • Rest time: 10 minutes
Yield: 2–4 servings

2 pounds or 2 loin chop racks of American lamb (4–5 bones each)

Salt and pepper to taste

½ cup butter, melted

½ cup hot sauce, such as Cholula

¼ cup chopped flat leaf parsley

1 clove fresh garlic, finely minced

½ teaspoon cracked black pepper

> **PAIR WITH:**
> - *Virgin Mary Mix (page 201)*
> - *Vanilla Panna Cotta with Citrus Caramel (page 147)*

* *If the chops are on the smaller side, roast 12 minutes plus 2 minutes under the broiler.*

Allow the lamb chops to come to room temperature, roughly 1 hour on the counter. Preheat oven to 475°. Line a baking sheet with foil or parchment. Season the lamb on both sides with salt and pepper, and place on the baking sheet. Mix melted butter, hot sauce, parsley, garlic, and pepper. Spoon half the prepared buffalo sauce over the lamb chops, and roast for 12 to 16 minutes*. For the final 2 minutes of cooking, switch your oven setting to broil to crisp the top of the lamb. This will yield a medium-rare lamb. Allow the lamb to rest 5 to 10 minutes before slicing. While the lamb is resting, assemble the salad.

Crunchy Celery and Blue Cheese Salad

Prep time: 10 minutes • Yield: 2–4 servings

2 cups thinly sliced celery

½ cup chopped flat leaf parsley

¼–½ cup blue cheese crumbles

2–3 tablespoons olive oil

Juice of half a lemon

Salt and pepper to taste

Gently mix all ingredients. Best served immediately.

Spicy, Fresh Heirloom Tomato Bucatini with Brie and Heirloom Tomato Toast

Spicy, Fresh Heirloom Tomato Bucatini

Prep time: 10 minutes • Cook time: 15–20 minutes • Yield: 4 servings

12 ounces dried bucatini*

¼ cup olive oil

3–4 cloves fresh garlic, smashed and chopped

2 anchovy fillets

1 teaspoon kosher salt

½ teaspoon cracked black pepper

¼ teaspoon crushed red pepper flakes

2 cups diced heirloom tomatoes

pasta cooking water, as needed

1 cup grated parmesan cheese

PAIR WITH:

♦ *Homemade Cold Brew with Brown Sugar Syrup (page 198), serve alongside dessert*

♦ *Noah's Apple Cake (page 175)*

* *Use spaghetti noodles if unable to find bucatini, roughly ¾ of a 16-ounce package of dried pasta.*

Cook the pasta according to package instructions. Heat a large skillet with tall sides over medium heat. Gently cook the olive oil, garlic, anchovies, salt, pepper, and pepper flakes until the garlic is fragrant and the anchovies have dissolved into the oil. Timing is important. As pasta is nearing al dente, add tomatoes to the oil and increase heat slightly. Add the al dente pasta to the skillet, and turn noodles in the sauce to coat. Add the pasta cooking water as needed to loosen the sauce. Turn off the heat and add all but two tablespoons of cheese. Gently toss pasta to melt cheese. Serve immediately. After plating, sprinkle remaining cheese on each plate.

Brie and Heirloom Tomato Toast

Prep time: 5 minutes • Cook time: 5 minutes • Yield: 8 pieces of toast

8 slices of artisan bread

1 13-ounce wheel Brie cheese

2–3 large heirloom tomatoes

Flaky sea salt

Set oven to broil. Lay the sliced bread on a baking sheet. Slice the Brie into roughly 16 even slices, and place 2 slices on each slice of bread. Broil until bread edges are golden brown and Brie is melted and bubbling, 2 to 4 minutes. This happens very quickly. It goes from perfect to burned in a matter of seconds, so pay careful attention. Slice each heirloom tomato into 4 ½-inch-thick rounds, totaling 8 rounds in all. Slice rounds in half, yielding 16 slices of tomato. Place 2 slices of tomato on each piece of toast. Drizzle with olive oil and sprinkle with salt. This is best eaten warm.

Melon with Basil and Prosciutto, Peach and Heirloom Tomato Panzanella, and Charcuterie and Cheese

This has to be one of my favorite easy summer meals. Mike and I enjoy these platters while watching TV or just visiting about the day. Make one of these or all three. These recipes pack up nicely for ladies' night or book club meeting.

Melon with Basil and Prosciutto

Prep time: 10 minutes • Yield: roughly 12 slices

1 medium-sized ripe cantaloupe

12–16 slices prosciutto

2 tablespoons olive oil

½ cup small (or torn) basil leaves

Flaky sea salt for garnishing

PAIR WITH:

- *Mom's Wine Punch (page 194)*
- *Strawberry Bellini (page 209)*
- *Molten Chocolate and Caramel Cakes (page 176)*

Slice the melon in half, and scoop and discard seeds. Slice the halves into at least 6 to 8 slices each side, and remove the rind. Wrap each slice of melon with a slice of prosciutto around the center. Drizzle with olive oil, and sprinkle with basil leaves and sea salt.

Peach and Heirloom Tomato Panzanella

Prep time: 10 minutes • Yield: 4–6 servings

OLIVE OIL CROUTONS

2–3 cups torn artisan bread

¼ cup olive oil

Sea salt to taste

PANZANELLA

3 slicing tomatoes, sliced into
½-inch rounds

2 ripe peaches, sliced

½ red onion, thinly sliced

2 cups cherry tomatoes, halved

1 cup torn sweet basil

¼ cup olive oil

¼ cup balsamic vinegar

Sea salt and pepper to taste

Begin with the croutons. Sauté the bread in olive oil until crisp and golden brown. Season with sea salt.

This salad is all about thoughtful layers. Place the sliced tomatoes on the bottom of a large platter or large, shallow bowl. Place the peaches, onions, and cherry tomatoes on top, then the torn basil. Sprinkle the croutons on top of that. Drizzle the olive oil and balsamic vinegar over top of that, and sprinkle with flaky sea salt and pepper.

Recipe continues on next page

Melon with Basil and Prosciutto, Peach and Heirloom Tomato Panzanella, and Charcuterie and Cheese

› Continued

Charcuterie and Cheese

Yield: serves 2–4 people

- 4 to 6 ounces triple-cream Brie cheese
- 8 ounces thinly sliced bresaola
- 8 ounces thinly sliced peppered salami
- 8 ounces thinly sliced mortadella
- 1 cup currants or fresh berries
- Crackers or crusty bread to serve along with

Arrange the meats around the cheese on a platter, then garnish with berries. The idea is to keep it simple and impressive. One or two kinds of cheese is ideal and affordable. Use any style of cured meats and your favorite cheese.

Lovely Toast x 3: Fresh Fig and Soft Cheese, Soft-Boiled Eggs and Green Beans with Hazelnut and Lemon Vinaigrette, and Chicken Caesar

This toast is a wonderful way to have a relaxed and delicious dinner that feels special but is really simple to prepare. Who knew that toast could be special? These three variations are delicious; make one, two, or all three!

Toast

Prep time: 15 minutes • Cook time: 15 minutes for all three variations
Yield: serves 2–4 people

PAIR WITH:

- *Hot Lemonade Tea (page 206), served iced*

- *Cream Coconut Cake (page 156)*

1 16-ounce loaf of artisan bread, cut into 12 even slices

½ cup olive oil
Sea salt for finishing

Use a large 12-inch skillet to fry the sliced bread in olive oil 1 tablespoon at a time over medium heat. Fry all 12 slices.

Fresh Fig and Soft Cheese

Yield: 3 servings

6 ripe fresh figs

6 ounces soft cheese of your choice (triple-cream Brie is delightful)

½ cup toasted, chopped hazelnuts
¼ cup honey

Spread 2 ounces of the soft cheese onto each of 3 slices of fried bread, then top with 2 sliced figs and one-third of the toasted hazelnuts. Drizzle finished toast with 1 tablespoon of honey.

Recipe continues on next page

Continued

Soft-Boiled Eggs and Green Beans with Hazelnut and Lemon Vinaigrette

Yield: 3 servings

¼ cup chopped hazelnuts

¼ cup olive oil

Juice and zest of 1 lemon

½ teaspoon Dijon mustard

Salt and pepper to taste

3 eggs

½ pound haricots verts (thin, tender French green beans)

Whisk together hazelnuts, olive oil, lemon juice and zest, mustard, salt, and pepper, and set aside.

Place three room-temperature eggs into a medium-sized saucepan with 4 cups water and bring to a boil. Add the green beans, and continue boiling for 7 minutes. Remove the green beans, and set them in an ice bath; this stops the cooking and sets their vibrant green color. Add the eggs to the same ice bath.

Gently peel the eggs, slice them, and set on toasts. Add one-third of the green beans to each slice of toast, and top with 1 to 2 tablespoons of vinaigrette.

Chicken Caesar

Yield: 3 servings

2 cups arugula

¼ cup prepared Caesar dressing
  (see recipe, page 117)

1 cup cooked chicken breast, cut
  into long strips

¼ cup shaved parmesan cheese

Toss the greens in the Caesar dressing in a mixing bowl. Add one-third of dressed greens to each piece of toast, and top with chicken and shaved parmesan.

Sweets

Have you ever cried into a key lime tart?

Sharing our lives has been my heart's calling since we started this journey in the food world. I share recipes, hopeful messages, and my experiences, and most of the time, I learn really beautiful and humbling life lessons through the process and through the people who grace our path. God speaks to my heart in the sweetest ways, and it's almost always with a recipe somehow attached.

Have you ever cried into a key lime tart? No? Is it only me who gets completely overwhelmed by gratitude at the thought of how wonderful this life is? It's not perfect, but it is remarkable. My husband, Michael, had a night job for fifteen years. He would wake up between one and three in the morning, depending on which route he was running that day, and he'd be gone sometimes until five in the evening. He'd then use his evenings, days off, and any time he could muster in between to start a food photography business from the ground up. This was the birth of Rustic Joyful Food. Seven years ago, when our restaurant closed and we had no direction, broken hearts, and a brand-new baby, Mike continued to work his night job. Our bills from the failed restaurant endeavor were crushing, and each time his paycheck was deposited, our bank accounts were red within hours. I remember setting an alarm for around 2:00 a.m. on paydays, packing Noah up, and crying the whole way to the ATM to withdraw just enough cash to get gas and groceries before all the bills were paid out.

This time in our lives was one of the most raw, but it was also beautiful. We were learning to love each other and depend on the Lord in a way we never had. I learned that hope had a real, tangible place in my life, and I learned we were strong. If not for this period of time, I fully believe my gritty side may never have been sharpened. I also think that if we'd never walked through those difficult times, I'd never have acquired this *desire* to share or an understanding of the value in sharing. There was healing in giving my time, my hope, and my stories, and especially in sharing food, even when we had very little. I now have a deep drive in my soul to share the love of Jesus and spread the idea that hope is very real. During this time in our lives, I promised Mike that one day, he'd only have one full-time job, and if we worked hard enough, it'd happen soon. Well, it took seven years, but we are now solely running Rustic Joyful Food together. We are grateful.

Recently, we traveled to Palm Springs following a rough couple of days when our little Milo was in the hospital. We stopped at a fast-food joint, and I ordered chicken strips and a key lime tart. Mike brought the food back to the car, and we had ourselves a little family car picnic. I took out the tart and had a bite. Wait. It was the best darn key lime tart I'd EVER TASTED! How could this be? The sign outside the restaurant said *Organic* accompanied by all the foodie buzzwords, but holy moly, this was good! I began to cry. My kiddos were munching on chicken, Mike was shoveling Cobb salad into his mouth, and tears were streaming down my face as I ate this pie. I took Mike's hand and said, "What we've always dreamed about is happening. Our business is thriving, we are sharing hope and delicious recipes with people, and I'm so proud of you." Mike is the backbone of our company. He works tirelessly to ensure deadlines are met, that photos look brilliant, that clients get exactly what they need, and more. He loves our babies in the most tender way possible no matter how tired the work makes him, and after six years of two full-time jobs, he was able to let one go. We were so blessed by that job, and it will always will be special to us.

All fresh starts are bittersweet, sort of like that pie. You will find the brilliantly simple lime tart recipe in this section along with dozens of other memory-making desserts. I think sometimes brilliant memories solidify in our hearts even as the moment is unfolding, and understanding this, our hearts grab on to everything right then, so as never to forget. The details stick: the smell, the slant of the sunlight, the taste of that sweet desert. These times, I believe, are God's little gifts to us, His aim to bring us right. Tap into that joy on a random day when you need a reminder of His mercies the most. These desserts are meant to grow tender memories in the hearts of those you make them for. Perhaps one day, when your sweet friend is recovering from a surgery and she samples a bit of Noah's Apple Cake, she will then always be reminded of how she was cared for. Maybe apples and cinnamon will trigger a heartfelt knowledge for the rest of her days that she is loved. Please never stop giving. Never stop sharing, and always bring dessert. The sweet is the balance to the bitterness we face in a life that is somehow always laced with joy, no matter what.

Apple Cinnamon Monkey Bread

Prep time: 20 minutes • Inactive resting time: 60 minutes • Bake time: 50 minutes • Yield: 1 standard Bundt cake, serves approximate 6 people

DOUGH

2 teaspoons quick yeast

1 cup warm milk

3 cups all-purpose flour

2 tablespoons butter, softened

2 tablespoons sugar

1 teaspoon kosher salt

1 egg

EXTRAS

1 cup sugar

2 tablespoons ground cinnamon

½ cup butter

1 cup applesauce

* *If dough is too wet, add flour 1 tablespoon at a time. If too dry, add warm milk 1 tablespoon at a time.*

** *At this point, if you have a bread machine, add remaining dough ingredients to the bread machine and choose the dough setting.*

Liberally butter and sugar a Bundt pan and set aside. Bloom the yeast in warm milk 5 minutes until foamy. Add to the bowl of a stand mixer with the remaining dough ingredients*. Use the dough hook to mix 6 to 7 minutes. This can also be done by hand. Allow the dough to rest 2 to 3 minutes, and knead again for 6 to 7 minutes**. Cover with a damp kitchen towel and allow to rise 45 minutes in a warm place or proofing drawer. Turn the dough out onto a lightly floured surface. Divide dough in half, then divide both halves in two. Repeat this process until you have 32 even pieces. Mix the sugar and cinnamon together in a shallow, wide bowl. Melt butter in another bowl. Dip the small pieces of dough in the melted butter, roll them in cinnamon sugar, and place into the Bundt pan, repeating the process until you've coated every piece of dough. After every third dough portion has been placed into the Bundt pan, add applesauce in 1 tablespoon increments to the pan until you've evenly distributed applesauce in and around the coated dough portions. Drizzle the remaining butter over top of the finished Bundt as well as any remaining cinnamon sugar. Preheat oven to 350° while you allow to proof 15 to 20 minutes. Bake 45 to 55 minutes. Allow to cool 5 minutes, then invert the pan onto a plate and enjoy. Best served warm.

Cherry Pie Bars

These bars aren't actually pie at all. This recipe makes a lovely, buttery pound cake intertwined with cherry pie filling. After many years of making this and calibrating it to fit my family's taste, I've come up with a glorious version I bring to absolutely every Fourth of July celebration.

Prep time: 10 minutes • Bake time: 35 minutes • Yield: 1 9×13-inch pan

1 cup butter, softened

2 cups sugar

4 eggs

2 cups all-purpose flour

1 teaspoon baking powder

½ teaspoon salt

1 (21-ounce) can cherry pie filling

Preheat oven to 350°. Cream the butter and sugar together in a stand mixer or with a hand mixer on low. Add the eggs one at a time. Beat until just combined. Add the flour, baking powder, and salt. Line a 9-by-13-inch pan with parchment paper. Spread a little over half the cake batter into the pan. Evenly spread the cherries over top, and spoon the rest of the cake batter over the cherries. It's fine if the cherries show through. Bake 35 minutes or until the top has turned slightly golden. Do not overbake. Allow to cool, and slice into squares. Enjoy!

Flaky Cream Biscuits

Prep time: 25 minutes • Bake time: 14 minutes • Yield: 12–18 biscuits, depending on cuts

3½ cups all-purpose flour

1 cup cold butter, diced into cubes

1 tablespoon baking powder

1 teaspoon kosher salt

2 cups cold heavy whipping cream

Preheat oven to 450°. Add the flour, butter, baking powder, and salt to the bowl of a stand mixer, and mix on low until butter is well incorporated but still in large chunks, a bit larger than a pea. Slowly pour the cold cream into buttery flour, and mix until it just comes together. Dough will be sticky. Turn the dough out onto a floured surface, and gently shape into a rectangle roughly 12 inches long and 2 inches thick. This is where your flaky layers begin. Fold biscuit dough just like a letter, a third down from the top, then another third from the bottom over and onto the first fold. Gently pat, roll out with a rolling pin, and fold once more. Repeat this process 6 times. On the final fold, roll dough out to a 6-by-12-inch rectangle about 2 inches thick. Slice into squares or cut into rounds, and bake 12 to 14 minutes or until biscuits are puffed, golden, and fully cooked. Serve with butter, honey, or raspberry jam!

Lime Tres Leches Cake

Lime Tres Leches Cake

Prep time: 10 minutes • Inactive time: 3 hours • Bake time: 35 minutes • Yield: 1 9×13-inch cake

LIME TRES LECHES CAKE

½ cup plus 2 tablespoons butter, softened

1 cup sugar

Zest of 1 lime

1 teaspoon vanilla extract

½ teaspoon kosher salt

5 large eggs or 4 XL eggs

1¾ cup all-purpose flour

2 teaspoons baking powder

¼ cup buttermilk

MILK DRENCH

1 cup whole milk

1 cup heavy cream

1 (14-ounce) can sweetened condensed milk

Juice of 1 lime

1 pinch salt

CREAM CHEESE WHIPPED CREAM

8 ounces cream cheese, softened

1½ cups heavy whipping cream

½ cup sugar

½ teaspoon vanilla extract

Zest of one lime

1 pinch salt

....

* *Do not over cream the butter and sugar by mixing faster than medium speed. Add the air as slowly as possible, then stop once cream is light and fluffy.*

Preheat oven to 350°. Line a 9-by-13-inch pan with parchment paper that's been lightly buttered. Cream the butter and sugar*, then add the lime zest, vanilla, and salt. With mixer on low, add the eggs. Only mix until eggs are just incorporated—do not overmix. Slowly add flour and baking powder in 2 additions by hand. Gently fold in the flour, then add the buttermilk. Spread the batter into your prepared pan, and bake for 22 to 28 minutes or until just baked. Do not overbake or cake will be dry, even after the milk is poured over. When cake is done, use a fork to poke dozens of holes all over the cake. The more holes, the better the opportunity you have to get the milk drench into all parts of the sponge. Add all milk drench ingredients to a bowl and whisk. Pour the milk drench evenly over the cake. Allow to sit at room temp for an hour before frosting.

Whip the softened cream cheese in a stand mixer until light and fluffy on medium to low speed. Slowly stream in heavy cream, sugar, vanilla, lime zest, and salt. Whip on medium speed until thickened, 4 to 5 minutes. Frost the cake, and refrigerate for at least 2 hours before serving. Cake is amazing the next day.

Pumpkin Tiramisu

142

Pumpkin Tiramisu

Active time: 20 minutes • Inactive time: 6–24 hours* • Yield: 1 9×13-inch pan, 12 servings

COFFEE SOAK

3 cups cold brew coffee

2 tablespoons instant coffee

2 teaspoons vanilla extract

1 pinch salt

CREAM LAYER

1 cup pumpkin purée, fresh
   or canned

16 ounces cream cheese, room
   temperature

2 cups heavy whipping cream

1 tablespoon bourbon

2 teaspoons vanilla extract

1 teaspoon ground cinnamon

½ teaspoon kosher salt

30 to 35 store-bought ladyfinger
   cookies

1 cup hot fudge sauce,
   warmed and pourable but not
   scalding hot

½ cup cocoa powder for
   dusting center and top of the
   finished pudding

*   *Best made a day in advance*

Prepare the coffee soak in a shallow bowl. Set aside.

Cream the pumpkin and cream cheese in the bowl of a stand mixer or with a hand mixer until smooth. Slowly stream in the whipping cream. Add the bourbon, vanilla, cinnamon, and salt. Beat on medium speed until whipping cream begins to thicken, leaving you with medium peaks. Do not overmix. Set aside.

Prepare your station: the coffee soak and a plate of cookies, the pumpkin cream, the warm fudge, and a 9-by-13-inch pan. Dunk a ladyfinger cookie into the coffee, then count to 1, flip, count to 1, and remove. Lay it quickly into the bottom of the pan. Repeat until the bottom is covered. Pour half of the pumpkin cream over the top of the soaked cookies. Drizzle the fudge over, then add a dusting of cocoa. Create a second layer on top of the fudge: soaked cookies, remainder of the pumpkin cream, a dusting of cocoa powder. Refrigerate for at least 6 hours; overnight is best. Enjoy!

Tender Gingerbread Cake

Prep time: 10 minutes • Bake time: 25–30 minutes • Yield: 1 9x9 square cake pan

- ½ cup plus 2 tablespoons butter, softened
- 1 teaspoon vanilla extract
- 1 cup packed muscovado sugar (dark brown works great)
- 2 eggs, room temperature
- ⅛ cup plain yogurt
- 2 cups all-purpose flour
- 1 teaspoon baking powder
- ½ teaspoon kosher salt
- ½ teaspoon cinnamon
- ¼ teaspoon ground cloves
- ¼ teaspoon ground ginger
- ¼ teaspoon apple pie spice
- ¾ cup molasses

GARNISHES
- ½ cup confectioners' sugar
- 1 cup pomegranate arils

Preheat oven to 350°F. Line the cake pan with parchment paper. Cream the butter, vanilla, and sugar on low speed for 3 minutes. Add the eggs one at a time and mix until just incorporated, then scrape down the sides of the bowl and gently fold the yogurt into the batter. In a separate bowl, whisk the flour, baking powder, salt, and spices together. In a third bowl, mix 1 cup hot water and molasses together. Now mix the dry ingredients into the batter in sections, alternating with the hot molasses mixture. Do not overmix. Pour the batter into your lined pan and bake for 25 to 30 minutes until the cake is well baked. Allow the gingerbread to cool, then dust with confectioners' sugar and pomegranate arils! This cake is also lovely with cream cheese icing!

Vanilla Panna Cotta with Citrus Caramel

Vanilla Panna Cotta with Citrus Caramel

Prep time: 5 minutes • Cook time: 25 minutes • Inactive time: 4 hours • Yield: 6 servings

PANNA COTTA

4 tablespoons cold water

1½ envelopes of gelatin

5 cups heavy cream

¾ cups sugar

2 teaspoons vanilla extract

1 pinch salt

CARAMEL

1 cup sugar

¼ cup heavy whipping cream

1 tablespoon butter

1 pinch salt

1 orange, zested and segmented

Mix the cold water and the gelatin, stir, and allow to sit. Heat the cream and sugar over medium heat in a large heavy-bottomed pot until the cream begins to steam—do not boil. Remove from the heat, and add the vanilla and salt. Add the gelatin, and stir to completely dissolve. Pour into 1-cup vessels and allow to cool for 4 hours before serving.

Heat the sugar without stirring over medium heat in a heavy-bottomed medium-sized saucepan. The sugar will begin to melt and bubble. Once it reaches a deep amber color but is not burned, remove from the heat, and add the cream, butter, vanilla, and salt. The caramel will seize and spatter, and this is fine. You may stir to incorporate everything at this point and add the orange zest and segments. Stir to mix the orange segments and zest in. This can be made in advance and stored at room temperature for 8 hours; refrigerate any leftover and warm before serving. Just before serving, spoon the caramel over the top of the fully chilled panna cotta.

Short-Crust Sour Cherry Cobbler

Prep time: 10 minutes • Cook time: 90 minutes • Yield: 1 7×10-inch crumble, 4–6 servings

FILLING

4–5 cups fresh or frozen pitted,
  tart cherries
2½ cups sugar
Juice and zest of 1 lemon
1 pinch salt
1 tablespoon cornstarch

CRUMBLE

1½ cups butter, softened
1½ cups all-purpose flour
½ cup sugar
1 pinch salt
½ cup cold cream

Preheat oven to 350°. Bring the cherries, sugar, lemon juice and zest, and salt to a simmer over medium heat. Remove ¼ cup of the hot syrup to a mug or glass measuring cup, and whisk in cornstarch to make a slurry. Pour the slurry into cherries, and cook 3 to 4 minutes or until the fruit syrup begins to thicken. Pour hot fruit into a 7-by-10-inch baking dish.

Mix the butter, flour, sugar, and salt in the bowl of your stand mixer until it begins to come together. Slowly add the cream, and stop mixer once ingredients just barely come together but still yield nice big crumbles. Place crumbles over cherries, and bake 40 to 60 minutes or until crumble is bubbling and crust is golden and lightly browned. Serve with vanilla ice cream (optional).

Double Peanut Marshmallow Treats

Prep time: 10 minutes • Cook time: 7 minutes • Yield: 1 9×13-inch pan of crispy treats, cuts in 12 or 24 squares easily

½ cup butter

15 ounces mini marshmallows

⅓ cup peanut butter

½ teaspoon kosher salt

2 teaspoons vanilla extract

6 cups crispy rice cereal

½ cup chopped, roasted, and
salted peanuts

Brown the butter in a large saucepan. This takes about 3 to 4 minutes over medium heat. Be very careful; it goes from brown to burned very quickly. Butter a 9-by-13-inch glass baking dish, and set aside. Once butter is brown, add marshmallows, peanut butter, and salt. Cook 2 to 3 minutes, then remove from heat and swirl in vanilla extract. Add cereal and chopped peanuts. Stir until just combined, and press into the buttered pan. Let stand 15 to 20 minutes before slicing. Add more chopped peanuts for garnish.

Apricot and Chocolate Rolls

Prep time: 10 minutes • Inactive time: 2 hours • Bake time: 30–40 minutes • Yield: 9 large rolls

DOUGH

2 teaspoons quick yeast

3 cups all-purpose flour

1 cup warm milk

2 tablespoons butter, softened

2 tablespoons granulated sugar

1 egg

1 teaspoon kosher salt

¼ cup brown sugar

FILLING

1 (16-ounce) jar warmed apricot
   jam

½ cup butter

1 pinch salt

1½–2 cups chopped dark
   chocolate

* *If the dough is too wet, add flour 1 tablespoon at a time. If too dry, add warm milk 1 tablespoon at a time.*

** *At this point, if you have a bread machine, add remaining dough ingredients to the bread machine and choose the dough setting.*

Add the yeast to the warm milk, and allow it to bloom for 5 minutes until foamy. Add to the bowl of a stand mixer* along with the remaining dough ingredients, except for brown sugar. Mix using the dough hook 6 to 7 minutes. This can also be done by hand. Allow the dough to rest 2 to 3 minutes, and knead again for 6 to 7 minutes**. Cover with a damp kitchen towel, and allow to rise 45 minutes in a warm place or proofing drawer. Once the dough is finished with its first rise, generously butter a 9-by-13-inch pan. Sprinkle the brown sugar evenly over the bottom of the pan.

Melt the jam, butter, and salt over medium heat, then remove from heat and allow to cool slightly. Mixture should not be hot when assembling the rolls, but warm is fine.

Turn the dough out onto a floured surface. Roll it out into a rectangle roughly 12 by 18 inches. Spread half the apricot jam and butter mixture over the surface of the dough. Pour the remaining jam mixture evenly into the bottom of the 9-by-13-inch pan. Sprinkle chopped dark chocolate evenly over the surface of the dough. Tightly roll the dough away from you so you have a nice log. Slice log into nine even rolls using a serrated knife. Preheat oven to 350°. Put the rolls into the pan, and allow to proof 20 to 25 minutes. Bake rolls 35 to 40 minutes.

Chocolate Chip Pumpkin Bread

Prep time: 10 minutes • Bake time: 30–35 minutes • Yield: 1 9×9-inch square loaf

½ cup butter, softened

1¾ cup brown sugar

2 tablespoons neutral oil

3 eggs, room temperature

1 cup pumpkin purée

2 teaspoons vanilla extract

1 teaspoon kosher salt

½ teaspoon ground cinnamon

1¾ cup all-purpose flour

1 tablespoon baking powder

½ tablespoon baking soda

1 (12-ounce) bag semisweet chocolate chips

½ cup full-fat buttermilk

Preheat oven to 350°. Generously butter and lightly flour a 9-by-9-inch baking pan, and set aside. Cream the butter and sugar on low speed, using a hand or stand mixer. Add the oil and then the eggs one at a time, mixing on low speed after each addition. Add the pumpkin, vanilla, salt, and cinnamon. Mix until just combined. Add the flour, baking powder, baking soda, and chocolate chips, mixing by hand gently until flour is just incorporated. Add the buttermilk last, and gently combine. Do not overmix. Pour batter into prepared baking pan and bake 25 minutes, then check the bread. Bake an additional 5 to 10 minutes or until bread is completely cooked but not overbaked.

Pineapple Cloud Cake

Prep time: 10 minutes • Bake time: 35 minutes • Yield: 1 9-inch cake pan

CAKE

1 box yellow cake mix

4 eggs

¼ cup sour cream

⅓ cup vegetable oil

1 (8-ounce) can crushed
pineapple and juice

7-MINUTE FROSTING

5 egg whites

2 cups sugar

1 teaspoon cream of tarter

½ teaspoon kosher salt

CAKE DECORATION

2 cups dried pineapple slices

Preheat oven to 350°. Mix all the cake ingredients, and pour into a buttered and floured 9-inch cake pan. Bake 30 to 35 minutes, until a toothpick comes out clean. Cool 20 minutes, then turn the cake out onto a cooling rack to cool completely. Use a serrated knife to gently slice the cake into two layers.

Combine all the frosting ingredients in a heavy-bottomed, scratch-resistant pot (such as an enamel cast iron). This frosting is best mixed with a hand mixer for 7 minutes on medium-low heat, until thick and beautiful ribbons begin forming. This is plenty of frosting for the layers (and sides, if you like).

To assemble the cake, put a dollop of the frosting on a serving plate; this serves as "glue." Place the first cake layer on top of the frosting. Gently smooth 1½ cups frosting onto the cake, spreading it to edges. Place the other layer on top. Cover top and sides with frosting. Decorate with dried pineapple.

Cream Coconut Cake

Prep time: 10 minutes • Bake time: 30–35 minutes • Yield: 1 9×9-inch pan

CAKE BATTER
2 cups flour
1½ teaspoons baking powder
½ teaspoon baking soda
1 teaspoon kosher salt
3 tablespoons butter, softened
⅓ cup light olive oil suitable for baking
1 vanilla bean, scraped
1½ cups granulated sugar
4 eggs
½ teaspoon coconut extract
1 teaspoon vanilla extract
½ cup sour cream
1 cup shredded coconut

ICING
1 (8-ounce) package cream cheese, softened
3 cups confectioners' sugar
2 tablespoons butter, softened
½ teaspoon coconut extract
Cream to thin icing, if needed
15 coconut cream candies (Raffaello brand works nicely)
1 cup sweetened shredded coconut

Preheat oven to 350°F. Combine flour, baking powder, baking soda, and salt in a large mixing bowl and whisk. Cream butter, oil, vanilla bean scrapings, and sugar in a separate bowl for 2 to 3 minutes on low speed. Add eggs one at a time. Add dry ingredients to the bowl, and fold extracts and sour cream into the batter. Do not over mix. Fold coconut in last. Spread batter into a generously buttered 9-by-9-inch pan for baking. Bake 30 to 35 minutes or until cake has risen, no longer wobbles in the center, and is golden. Cool completely before icing.

Mix cream cheese, confectioners' sugar, butter, and extract until smooth and creamy. Add a splash of cream to thin if necessary. Add cream in teaspoon increments, as it can get thin very quickly. Spread frosting over top of the cake, and decorate with coconut cream candies and sprinkled shredded coconut. Enjoy!

Creamy Lime Tart

Creamy Lime Tart

Prep time: 10 minutes • Bake time: 15 minutes • Yield: 1 9-inch pie

CRUST

12 shortbread cookies, crushed

2–3 tablespoons butter, melted

FILLING

1 (14-ounce) can sweetened
   condensed milk

3 egg yolks

2 whole eggs

¾ cup lime juice, roughly 3–4
   juicy limes

¼ cup sugar

1 tablespoon lime zest

1 pinch kosher salt

SOFT WHIPPED CREAM

2 cups heavy cream

¼ cup sugar

Preheat oven to 375°. Combine the crushed shortbread cookies with melted butter. Press into 9-inch tart pan, making sure to come up the sides of the pan. Whisk all the filling ingredients until smooth and creamy. Pour into your tart pan, and bake 15 minutes. Remove the tart from oven, and allow to cool completely. Whip the cream and sugar until soft peaks form, then top the tart with soft whipped cream to serve. This is best served cold.

Basic Not-Basic Chocolate Cream Pie

Prep time: 15 minutes • Bake time: 10 minutes • Yield: 1 9- or 10-inch pie

CRUST

13 graham crackers

6 tablespoons butter, melted

PIE FILLING

2½ cups heavy cream

½ cup whole milk

1 (3.4-ounce) package all-natural instant chocolate pudding

1 tablespoon unsweetened cocoa powder

1 teaspoon vanilla extract

WHIPPED CREAM TOP

1½ cups heavy whipping cream

3 tablespoons confectioners' sugar

½ teaspoon vanilla extract

Preheat oven to 350°. Crush graham crackers, and mix with melted butter. This should resemble wet sand when perfectly mixed. Press crumbs into a 9- or 10-inch pie plate, and bake for 10 minutes. Remove from the oven, and place directly into the freezer for five minutes. Whip pie filling ingredients with a hand or stand mixer until creamy and slightly fluffy. Spoon pudding into the graham cracker crust. Mix whipped cream ingredients in the same bowl pudding was mixed in. Spoon over top of the pudding, and refrigerate two hours or overnight before serving. I like to allow the pie to sit at room temp 15 to 20 minutes before serving. Garnish with fresh berries and enjoy!

Magic Shell and Pistachio Sundaes

Prep time: 10 minutes • Yield: 4 servings

1 cup dark chocolate chips or
 discs
2–3 tablespoons unrefined
 coconut oil*
1 tablespoon unsweetened cocoa
 powder

1 teaspoon vanilla extract
1 pinch sea salt
2 pints vanilla ice cream
¾ cup toasted pistachios

> * *Feel free to use refined coconut oil if you don't want a prominent coconut undertone in your magic shell.*

Melt chocolate and coconut oil in 30-second bursts in a wide-mouth mason jar or microwave-safe bowl. Mix until smooth; generally, it takes no more than a minute. You may also use a double boiler. Add the cocoa powder, vanilla, and salt, then mix. Spoon the warm magic shell over vanilla ice cream, and sprinkle with the toasted pistachios. Also makes an excellent coating for cold fruit or bonbons.

Chocolate Peanut Butter Tart

Chocolate Peanut Butter Tart

Prep time: 15 minutes • Bake time: 28 minutes • Yield: 1 10-inch tart

CRUST

9 whole graham crackers

1 tablespoon unsweetened cocoa powder

1 tablespoon sugar

3 tablespoons butter, melted

FILLING

1 cup creamy peanut butter

¼ cup sugar

1 (14-ounce) can sweetened condensed milk

3 egg yolks

½ cup heavy cream

2 teaspoons vanilla extract

¼ teaspoon salt

TOPPING

1 cup semisweet chocolate chips

¼ cup heavy cream

¼ cup chopped salted peanuts

Flaky sea salt (optional)

Preheat the oven to 350°. Blitz the graham crackers, cocoa powder, and sugar in your food processor until a fine and crumbly crust comes together. If you don't have a food processor, crush the mixture in a freezer bag using the bottom of a drinking glass or rolling pin. Add the butter and mix. Press mixture into the bottom of a 9- or 10-inch tart pan with removable bottom. If you don't have a tart pan, a pie dish works just fine. Bake 10 minutes, remove from oven, and allow to cool slightly.

Combine the peanut butter, sugar, condensed milk, and egg yolks, and mix until smooth. Add the cream, vanilla, and salt, and mix again. Tip: Before pouring the prepared peanut butter filling into your tart pan or pie dish, spray a touch of nonstick cooking spray along the inner rim of the prepared crust. This prevents the filling from sticking to the sides of the pan when it's finished baking. Pour the filling into the crust, and bake 15 to 18 minutes. The center should have a slight wobble still. This tart is finished before it looks completely done. Allow to cool completely before adding the topping.

Melt the chocolate and heavy cream in 30 second blitzes in the microwave, then add the cream, and mix until smooth. Pour the chocolate over the cooled tart, and sprinkle with the chopped salted peanuts and flaky sea salt.

Chocolate Almond Coconut Granola Sundae

Prep time: 10 minutes • Bake time: 30 minutes • Inactive time: 45–60 minutes
Yield: 6 cups of granola (roughly 18 servings)

> Sharing tip: Think you can't share ice cream? Think again! There's nothing sweeter than packing up an ice cream sundae treat to drop off at a loved one's home. Simply pack the ice cream, granola, and toppings into separate containers, write a lovely note, drop it off, and head out.

GRANOLA

3 cups rolled oats

1¼ cups unsweetened large coconut flakes

¾ cup sliced almonds

½ cup cocoa nibs

½ cup unpacked brown sugar

⅓ cup unrefined coconut oil or butter, melted

⅓ cup almond butter

1 teaspoon vanilla extract

½ teaspoon ground cinnamon

1 teaspoon Himalayan pink salt

1 beaten egg white

SUNDAE

2 pints vanilla ice cream

½ cup prepared caramel sauce

2 cups prepared whipped cream

Preheat oven to 300°. Mix all the ingredients except the egg white in a bowl. Add beaten egg white as a binder. Spread onto a parchment-lined baking sheet, and bake until granola begins to pick up a lovely golden color, about 25 to 30 minutes. Allow to cool completely before breaking it up into clumps. Store in an airtight container for up to 2 weeks.

Assemble sundaes by scooping the ice cream evenly into 4 bowls. Top with ¼ cup granola, caramel sauce, and whipped cream.

This recipe will yield leftover granola, which is perfect because in addition to being a delightful ice cream topper, granola serves triple duty as a breakfast, snack, and dessert.

Wild Dried Blueberry Pound Cake

Prep time: 15 minutes • Bake time: 45 minutes • Yield: 1 9×9-inch square cake or 2 9-inch loafs

CAKE

1½ cups granulated sugar

1 cup butter, softened

¼ cup sour cream, room
 temperature

2 tablespoons olive oil

1 teaspoon vanilla extract

½ teaspoon kosher salt

3 eggs, room temperature

2 cups all-purpose flour

1½ cups dried blueberries

2 teaspoons baking powder

GLAZE

1 cup confectioners' sugar

Juice of 1 lemon

Preheat oven to 350°. Generously butter a 9-by-9-inch square cake pan or 2 9-inch loaf pans, and set aside. Mix the sugar, butter, sour cream, oil, vanilla, and salt on low speed until light and fluffy. Mix the eggs into the mixture one at a time, being sure not to overmix. Add the flour, blueberries, and baking powder, and gently fold by hand until it's just come together. Spoon the batter into pan(s), and bake 35 to 45 minutes or until cake is set. Allow cake to cool slightly before glazing.

Make the glaze by mixing sugar and lemon juice. Drizzle over top of the cake.

Churros con Chocolate

Prep time: 5–8 minutes • Cook time: 15 minutes • Yield: roughly 1 dozen 5- to 7-inch churros

CINNAMON-SUGAR DREDGE

1 cup granulated sugar

2 tablespoons sparkling sugar
   (optional)

1 teaspoon ground cinnamon

¼ teaspoon kosher salt

BATTER

¼ cup granulated sugar

2 tablespoons butter

1 teaspoon kosher salt

1 teaspoon orange zest (optional)

1¾ cups all-purpose flour

1 teaspoon vanilla extract

6 cups canola oil

CHOCOLATE SAUCE FOR DIPPING

1½ cups bittersweet chocolate

1 tablespoon butter

Set up 2 large shallow bowls, one with the cinnamon-sugar dredge ingredients mixed together and one with paper towels to drain the cooked churros. Set aside.

Mix sugar, butter, salt, and orange zest with 2 cups water in a saucepan, bring to a boil, and remove from heat. Stir the flour and vanilla into the water until completely mixed and pulling away from the sides of the pan. Let the batter stand for 15 to 20 minutes, until cool to the touch. Load the batter into a pastry bag with a large star tip (we used a Wilton #9). In lieu of a pastry bag, load batter into a plastic freezer bag, and cut a ¾-inch tip off the bottom corner. Bring oil to 375° in a pot safe for frying. Pipe 5- to 7-inch sections of batter into hot oil, and fry 5 to 8 minutes, until churros are golden brown. Drain churros briefly on the paper towel, and roll in the cinnamon-sugar dredge, repeating with the rest of the batter. Melt the chocolate and butter in 30-second bursts in a microwave. Stir until smooth and glossy. Pour into a small bowl, and use for dunking. Store any uneaten churros in an airtight container.

Olive Oil and Espresso Dark Chocolate Cake with Cream Cheese Buttercream and Caramel

Olive Oil and Espresso Dark Chocolate Cake

Prep time: 10 minutes • Bake time: 24–28 minutes • Yield: 1 9×13-inch cake

- 2 cups all-purpose flour
- 1¾ cups sugar
- ½ cup cocoa powder
- 1½ teaspoons baking powder
- 1 teaspoon kosher salt
- ½ teaspoon baking soda
- 4 ounces bittersweet chocolate chips, melted
- 1 cup half-and-half or heavy cream
- ½ cup olive oil
- 3 eggs
- 1 teaspoon vanilla extract
- 1 cup boiling hot espresso or strong coffee

Preheat oven to 350°. Butter and flour a 9-by-13-inch baking dish. Combine all the dry ingredients in a mixing bowl, and whisk to combine. Add all the remaining ingredients except boiling espresso. Stir gently until ingredients are just mixed together. Add boiling espresso, and stir to combine. The batter will be thin. Pour batter into your prepared pan. Bake 20 to 25 minutes or until cake is done. Allow cake to cool completely before frosting.

Cream Cheese Buttercream and Caramel

Prep time: 10 minutes • Bake time: 24–28 minutes • Yield: 1 9×13-inch cake

- 3½ cups confectioners' sugar
- 1 (8-ounce) package cream cheese, room temperature
- ½ cup butter, softened
- 1 teaspoon vanilla extract
- 8 ounces prepared caramel sauce

Place everything except caramel into a mixing bowl. Mix frosting until smooth and creamy. A hand mixer works great for this.

Frost the cooled cake with cream cheese buttercream. Drizzle caramel over top. Slice and serve.

Apple Cranberry Shortbread Crumble

Prep time: 20 minutes • Bake time: 60–75 minutes • Yield: 1 9×13-inch pan (serves 8–12 people)

1 (14-ounce) package fresh cranberries

2 cups loosely packed brown sugar

1 cup apple cider or juice (no sugar added)

½ teaspoon ground cinnamon

1 pinch kosher salt

3 Granny Smith apples, peeled, cored, and thinly sliced

2 Fuji apples, peeled, cored, and thinly sliced

2 Gala apples, peeled, cored, and thinly sliced

SHORTBREAD CRUMBLE

1½ cups butter, softened

1 cup granulated sugar

1 pinch kosher salt

2½ cups all-purpose flour

Preheat your oven to 350°. Bring the cranberries, brown sugar, cider, cinnamon, and salt to a boil over medium heat in a large, heavy-bottomed saucepan. Cook 5 to 7 minutes until cranberries have burst and the juice has thickened slightly. Remove from heat. Place apples into saucepan with cranberry syrup, and stir to coat. Set aside.

Make the crumble by placing the butter, sugar, and salt into the bowl of your stand mixer and creaming ingredients with speed set to low. Add the flour, and mix slowly until crumbly and it's just come together.

Butter a glass 9-by-13-inch baking dish. Place fruit in the bottom of the baking dish, and cover evenly with the shortbread crumble.

Bake 60 to 75 minutes or until crust is golden brown, apples are cooked completely, and juices have thickened. If crumble top begins to brown too quickly, place a sheet of foil loosely over the top to prevent overbrowning. Spoon warm crumble and pan sauce over vanilla ice cream.

One-Pan Lava Cake

Noah's Apple Cake

Prep time: 15 minutes • Bake time: 30 minutes • Yield: 1 9 x 13-inch cake

3 eggs, room temperature

½ cup butter, melted

½ cup vegetable oil

2 cups all-purpose flour

2 cups dark brown sugar

2 teaspoons vanilla extract

1 teaspoon kosher salt

½ teaspoon baking soda

½ teaspoon ground cinnamon

4 apples, peeled and diced
(honey crisp, Fuji, and Granny
Smith work well)

Preheat oven to 350°. Generously butter a 9-by-13-inch pan. Whip eggs, butter, and oil until foamy. Add flour, brown sugar, vanilla, salt, baking soda, and cinnamon. Mix until it just comes together, then fold in the apples and pour into baking dish. Bake until set, about 30 minutes.

One-Pan Lava Cake

Prep time: 10 minutes • Cook time: 40 minutes • Yield: 1 8×10-inch cake

3 eggs

1 cup sugar

½ cup butter, melted

1 (11-ounce) bag dark chocolate
chips

2 teaspoons vanilla extract

2–3 tablespoons all-purpose flour

2 tablespoons unsweetened dark
cocoa powder

½ teaspoon kosher or Himalayan
salt

Vanilla ice cream (optional)

Store-bought fudge (optional)

Preheat oven to 350°. Generously butter a 9-inch round or 8-by-10-inch baking dish. Beat the eggs and sugar at low speed in the bowl of a stand mixer (or by hand) until light and fluffy, 5 or 6 minutes. The sugar will have lost much of its gritty texture but not all of it. Pour the melted butter over the chocolate chips and stir to melt the chocolate and combine. Pour melted chocolate into the egg mixture along with the vanilla, and mix until just combined. Gently fold in the dry ingredients, roughly 4 to 6 turns by hand. Pour the batter into the prepared dish, and bake 18 to 24 minutes, depending on the size of the dish. Look for set edges and a wobbly center. The cake will have a cracked and just barely set middle. Overbaking will result in no lava. Optionally, serve with vanilla ice cream and hot fudge.

Molten Chocolate and Caramel Cakes

Prep time: 7–8 minutes • Bake time: 10–12 minutes • Yield: 4 8-ounce half pint jars or 8 4-ounce ramekins

1 (11½-ounce) bag of 60% semisweet chocolate chips

½ cup butter

3 eggs, room temperature

⅓ cup sugar

¼ cup all-purpose flour

1 teaspoon vanilla extract

½ teaspoon kosher salt

1 (8-ounce) jar prepared salted caramel sauce for garnish

Preheat oven to 375°. Butter and flour your chosen vessels. We used four 8-ounce wide-mouth jars. Microwave the chocolate and butter for 1 minute (in two 30-second bursts to prevent popping), then mix until chocolate is melted and completely incorporated into butter. Cream eggs and sugar in the bowl of a stand mixer on low speed. Add the chocolate and butter to the eggs and sugar, and mix until it just comes together. Add the flour, vanilla, and salt. Fold the batter by hand until no more flour is visible. Do not overmix. Divide batter evenly between your prepared dishes, and place on a small baking sheet. Bake 8 to 10 minutes until the tops of the cakes are no longer glossy but not cooked in the center. Remove the cakes from the oven, and run a knife along their edges before inverting onto a plate. Place 1 to 2 tablespoons of prepared salted caramel sauce over top of each cake.

Apple Butter Crumb Cake

Prep time: 10 minutes • Bake time: 45–55 minutes • Yield: 9×9-inch baking pan

CAKE

1 cup butter, softened

1¼ cup granulated sugar

1 tablespoon olive oil

1 teaspoon kosher salt

1 teaspoon vanilla extract

3 eggs, room temperature

⅓ cup sour cream, room
  temperature

2 cups all-purpose flour

1½ teaspoons baking powder

½ cup pecan apple butter

CRUMBLE TOPPING

¼ cup butter, softened

⅓ cup all-purpose flour

⅓ cup granulated sugar

¼ teaspoon baking powder

1 pinch salt

CINNAMON CREAM GLAZE

1½ cups confectioners' sugar

¼–⅓ cup heavy cream

1 teaspoon ground cinnamon

1 pinch salt

Preheat oven to 350°. Line a 9-by-9-inch square baking pan with parchment paper. Slowly cream the butter and sugar until light and fluffy. Add the olive oil, salt, vanilla, and one egg at a time, mixing until it just comes together with each additional egg. Add the sour cream, then gently fold in the flour and baking powder. Spread the batter into the lined pan. Spoon the pecan apple butter in even dollops over the batter. Drag a butter knife through the pecan apple butter and batter to create swirls. Combine all the crumble topping ingredients in a bowl, and mash with a fork until it resembles a crumbly dough. Sprinkle the crumbles over top of the cake, and bake 45 to 55 minutes. Prepare the cinnamon cream glaze by mixing all ingredients in a bowl until smooth. Drizzle the glaze over top of the warm cake.

Caramelized Banana Cream Pudding

Prep time: 15 minutes • Chill time: 2 hours • Yield: 1 9-inch pie, approximately 6 servings

15 shortbread cookies, crushed
1 (5.1-ounce) box of your favorite
    instant vanilla pudding

2 cups heavy cream
1 cup whole milk
1 teaspoon vanilla extract

3 bananas
3 tablespoons sugar

Crush the cookies in a gallon-sized freezer bag. Whisk the vanilla pudding mix, cream, milk, and vanilla extract in a large mixing bowl until smooth, then set aside. Place one-third of the crushed cookies in the bottom of a 9-inch pie plate. Slice one banana into thin rounds, and place on top of the cookies. Cover cookie crumbs and bananas with half the pudding. Sprinkle another third of the cookie crumbs over top of the pudding layer. Repeat this process once more, until all the pudding and crumbs have been used. Chill the pudding two hours before serving. When the pudding is ready to serve, prepare the remaining two bananas. Set oven to broil, and line a baking sheet with parchment paper. Slice bananas on the bias, and lay on the parchment paper. Sprinkle a layer of sugar over bananas, and broil 3 to 4 minutes or until sugar caramelizes. Take bananas from the oven and remove from the parchment one at a time, using a spoon. Bananas will be very soft, so be gentle. Place them on top of the finished pudding.

Drinks

I am a forager at heart.

When Noah was about three, I'd drive to my sister's house throughout summer, whenever I had a day off from work. I wanted my sweet boy to be close to his cousins, so we would pack up the car and make the two-hour trek south for visits whenever possible. We'd play and visit for most of the day, until it was time to make the drive back up north. Just around the corner from my sister's home, there was a small farm with plenty of horses in the back, stables, and a few massive, beautiful fruit trees out in the side pastures.

Now, I am a forager at heart. By forager, I mean I'll find any berry bush to pick from or flower plant to cut or fruit tree to harvest from, to a fault. My poor husband, at my gentle nudging, has been known to climb into some unusual places to see if that fruit tree has delicious and edible fruits or to saunter into the park with scissors to chop the peonies down and bring them home to decorate. We've driven at strange hours to the homes of many acquaintances to claim bags from doorsteps designated for the lady from the internet! People familiar with my desire for harvested goods have offered me fruit from their yards for as long as I can remember, and I like to repay them with a jar or two of jam or a pie.

The pastures of this particular farm looked a bit overgrown. The main house's paint was chipped, and the fences looked as though they needed mending and TLC. In driving by often, I began to notice one of the fruit trees loaded with golden fruit. Were they plums? Were they peaches or apricots? Each time we'd make the drive, I'd see the fruit was bolder and heavy, just falling off the tree. This amount of fruit needed harvesting, and soon! I'd say to Noah, "Do you think we should stop and ask to pick some?" He'd invariably say, "Yes, Mama! Stop! Oh, please, I want to see the horses." But each time, I'd continue past, not wanting to bother the tree's owner.

One day, though, I noticed the lower branches dropping so much fruit, I couldn't resist the temptation to stop in and ask. I was a little nervous. It was just me and my sweet boy and an old home that felt like it may not want company. It was hot outside. We parked and knocked on the door. Noah was so excited. A weathered man of about eighty answered the door with a snarl. "What can I do

Sometimes, all we need to do is step outside the polite, arm's-length social norm and visit with somebody a little to change their day.

for you?" he said unwelcomingly. I wanted to run, yelling over my shoulder, "Uh, wrong house, sorry!" But I didn't waver. I said, "I can't help but notice that tree. It's loaded with fruit." He cut me off: "Yes!" I said, "Can we pick some?" His demeanor changed from irritable to curious. "What? You want to pick those plums? I think you're too late! They were at their peak last week." I said, "Oh gosh, well, I'm sorry to bother you. We'll let you go."

As I turned to walk away, clutching Noah's hand, he called out, "Well, if you'd give me a minute, I'll walk out to the pasture with you, and maybe we can find some for you and your boy."

Success! Five minutes later, he was in a much easier mood, leading the way with a long, tired gait. He made small talk and asked Noah how his day was. We got out to the tree, and there were indeed some good golden plums left. He reached up and pulled branches down for us to pick from, and he talked about all the plum wine he'd made from this tree over the years. He talked about how the horses loved to eat the plums right off the tree most years and how, once the fruit dropped, they wanted nothing to do with it. By this time, he almost seemed lighter as he spoke. The stories he told us—about his horses and how, nowadays, he mostly boarded horses for others and how his little farm got started—brought him joy.

Once we filled an old cookie tin with the plums, he looked at me and said, "Would you two like to pat the horses?" Normally, I'd never wander around a stranger's home or property, but I felt it would be okay this day. Much to Noah's delight, we walked back to the barn to pat Bubbles and China. While we visited the horses, he told about a time the whole batch of plum wine was no good. He said he sure wished he had some to send along with me. Then he said, "I've missed it this summer, but maybe I'll make a batch next year." When our short visit was over, he bid us farewell.

Noah is now eight, and my sister has since moved away from that little spot, but from time to time, he'll ask about those horses. I think about that man and how our visit was quite unexpected and broke into his routine enough to bring joy. That twenty minutes was an authentic expression of community. I didn't learn his name, but I knew that he felt known after we left. I don't hear of

plum wine too often, but when I do, I think of him and his horses and his beautiful tree filled up with fruit.

Sometimes, all we need to do is step outside the polite, arm's-length social norm and visit with somebody a little to change their day. In this section, you will find all kinds of beverages to enjoy while communing. There are brandies and liqueurs, homemade and inspired. There are simple cocktails and sips to laugh over, warm and comforting. All these drinkable delights are worthy of sending along with someone you love or dropping on a doorstep as a pleasant surprise.

So next time you see a loaded fruit tree, maybe stop in and ask to pick some. You may just share a little joy with someone who needs it.

Homemade Limoncello

Prep time: 15 minutes • Inactive time: 3 months • Yield: roughly 1 ½ quarts

This is excellent for summer sipping, chilled in your favorite lemon cocktail, or drizzled over a buttery lemon cake!

6 organic lemons

1 (750 mL) bottle vodka

2 cups sugar

Wash lemons and pat dry. Using a vegetable peeler, peel zest from lemons in long strips, leaving the white pith behind. Juice three of the lemons into a large jar, add zest, and cover with vodka—a 30-ounce Weck jar works well for this. Cover with a tightly fitted lid, and store three months in a cool, dark place. After three months, strain the mixture through a fine mesh sieve. Discard the zest. Bring sugar and 2 cups water to a boil, then remove from heat and cool completely. Combine the infused vodka with the cooled simple syrup, and store in jars indefinitely in a cool, dry place.

Crème de Cassis

Crème de Cassis

In my dating days—my early twenties—I was a proud member of Match.com. I prided myself on how many dates I could go on. My girlfriends and I decided we'd go on every date for at least a month for the stories alone. I mean, they were pure gold!

One guy dressed in a wool three-piece suit when it was ninety-five degrees outside and, while sweating profusely, asked how many children I'd like to have. Before I could even order an appetizer! *Kids? Um, how 'bout we start with egg rolls?* Another guy told me he was thirty-three, which was a stretch for my twenty-three-year-old self, and he showed up and was like, "Welp, as you can tell, I'm not thirty-three. I'm thirty-eight." *Try fifty-eight, buddy. NEXT!* And so on and so on.

I'd laugh with my girlfriends about the adventure and say yes to the next date. By the end, I'd met a guy who was nice. No sparks but nice. He was awkward and kind and an attorney. Extra mom points for guys with great jobs, am I right? But this guy was a dud for me. No charisma and zero fun. He'd shush me if I laughed too loud at dinner and cut me off to talk about himself. I can remember prank calling him with my girlfriends and just laughing and laughing with our fake Russian accents, asking him if he'd checked in for his flight. Harmless fun, but he didn't laugh; he was annoyed.

Since I was little, my mom has asked if I'd like the $10.95 pants now or if I'd like to wait and save for the well-made, incredible designer pants. This has been a metaphor I've lived by for the last twenty years. In life and jobs and even my marriage. That nice attorney was the perfect example of what I wanted at the moment but not the best thing for the long run. That guy was $10.95 pants (no offense to you, kind sir, wherever you may be).

We all love low-cost clothes that still look good, but often, after three to four washes, when they start to lose their shape or they fray, the love affair is over. For some reason, I can buy a pair of $10 tights ten times a year but struggle to purchase a $60 pair that fits incredibly and will last me two years. And there it is, my mom's voice in my head asking if I want to buy pants for $10.95 my whole life or if I'd like to wait and save up for those $120 jeans that become like an old friend for years. I'd choose the latter now. I'd take those glorious jeans that cost a fortune because they'll be better in the long run.

For the past twenty years, every so often when I want something to happen yesterday—a contract; a job; in my dating years, a relationship; now, to fix issues in my marriage; a big break; even a recipe to turn out while cutting fifteen steps—I can hear my mom gently urging me to consider $10.95 pants or waiting on God's best. You see, it's tough to not want the crumbs now. The relationship, the quick fix, the all-fat diet to acquire that smoking body. But I want the long run, the better bet, the fight for the best. After the long haul and waiting out that dream to come to fruition, I've never thought, *Well, sooner would have been better.* The timing is always perfect, even it was a slog to get there. Good often takes time, but the best is absolutely a lengthy labor of love and hard work. It's always worth those hours and weeks and years it takes to get to the glory. This is often how God works in our lives. He is absolutely a God of instant miracles in some cases, but oftentimes, he loves us enough to teach us and point us to the glory due us in the waiting.

So while researching cassis recipes, I found dozens of methods. Some added wine and more sugar, curing in the dark. Some removed the stems and tails and mashed with no heat. Some recipes called for heating the mixture and allowing it to sit in the sun for up to four weeks; others preferred the temperature to be much cooler and recommended aging in the fridge only. There were several recipes that said to let it sit overnight and enjoy!

I wanted fast results; I had no time to wait. The other morning, I was setting out to make the liqueur, and I was determined to utilize the fastest method. When I started the mash and placed it in its jars, I thought, *This is so beautiful, quite expensive, and I would hate to miss out on something great because I chose to rush the process.* I don't want $10.95 pants—I'm worth designer jeans, folks. So I opted to wait.

After three months, I'm happy to say I have the most exquisite liqueur, perfectly preserved with time and patience and love. Loved ones will be impressed with your unbelievably delicious cocktails and marvel at the wonderful agedness of it all.

Crème de Cassis

Prep time: 30 minutes • Inactive time: 2–3 weeks • Yield: roughly 1 ½ quarts

4 pints red and black currants (about 5 cups)

2 cups sugar

1 (750 mL) bottle vodka

Mash currants, stems included, with sugar until it's dissolved. Stir in vodka, and mix thoroughly. Pour the mash into 2 quart-size jars fitted with lids, and store in a cool, dark place 2 to 3 weeks.

Strain through cheesecloth, and bottle for keeping. The liqueur should last indefinitely. Use in champagne cocktails, as an after-dinner liqueur, or pour over panna cotta.

Irish Cream Mason Jars to Go

Let's rethink gift-able food. Mason jars make incredible containers for premixed cocktail bases. They take up very little space, and I think people are genuinely surprised and delighted when a delicious mason jar cocktail shows up alongside the tray bake of pasta or roast. The truth is, we all need a break; we all need to be cared for. And when delivering a food gift, if you've taken into account all these small details, it goes quite a long way in showing love.

I've delivered these simple and delicious Irish coffee creams in jars to several friends, usually with a meal also in tow. One of my friends had her fifth baby, and she and her hubby were over-the-moon excited to pour an Irish coffee cream over ice and devour beer-braised pot roast while their babies slept. Another friend, who was ill, once opened her front door in her pajamas to find me standing there with these mason jar beauties and a potpie; she cried, overjoyed.

Truth is, sometimes life gets unwieldy, loud, and overfull, but it's so good. When you hand deliver a mason jar that reads *just add ice*, that person feels special. No muddling, no shaking, no work necessary. Just relax in your living room alone, or not, with zero expectations, and enjoy the moment. That's really what a cocktail is for: slowing down time and savoring the moment. Every so often, for just a moment, we must ignore the laundry that needs putting away and bathrooms that need scrubbing.

This season, pack a few jars and drop 'em off with those folks you love.

Yield: 1-quart mason jar, about 8–10 cocktails

1 cup Kahlua coffee liqueur

1 cup Irish cream liqueur

2 cups heavy cream

2 teaspoons vanilla extract

1 pinch sea salt

Pour all ingredients into a quart-sized mason jar, place the lid on, and gently shake to combine. Keep chilled 2 to 3 days. Serve over ice or in iced coffee.

Mom's Wine Punch

Muddled blueberries, limeade, and seltzer water equal a pretty good time. My parents moved out to a lake about seven years ago. For our family, summertime isn't just warm weather and relaxed attitudes anymore; it's like a vacation every time you walk through my parents' doors! My mother has a new lease on life. She is more relaxed, always up for a party. "Wine punch?" she'll say, and everyone will reply, "Yes, of course!" Whichever white wine you have on hand works like a charm.

Prep time: 10 minutes • Yield: just under 2 quarts

2 cups fresh blueberries
2 cans lime seltzer or lime club
  soda
1 lime, sliced

1 (750 mL) bottle chilled,
  dry white wine (pinot grigio
  or sauvignon blanc work
  wonderfully)
3 cups prepared limeade

Optional: any fruit you have on
  hand, such as watermelon,
  strawberries, pitted cherries,
  or any summer fruit makes a
  delicious addition

Combine blueberries, seltzer water, and lime in a 2-quart pitcher. Use a wooden spoon to crush and muddle the berries with the lime. Cover with wine and limeade, then serve over ice.

Pear Brandy

This brandy makes the most delicious sipping liqueur or champagne cocktail during the fall.

Prep time: 10 minutes • Inactive time: 8–10 days • Yield: a little over 1 quart

3 ripe pears

3 cups brandy

1 cup sugar

Slice pears, and place them in a quart jar. Cover the fruit with brandy. If you do not have brandy, whiskey or bourbon works well. Cover with a nonreactive lid, and place in a cool, dry place 8 to 10 days. Strain the mixture through a fine mesh sieve. Bring sugar and 1 cup water to a boil in a medium-sized saucepan, making a simple syrup. Allow syrup to cool completely, and add to the strained brandy, gently stirring to combine. This keeps beautifully for up to one year in a cool, dark place or the refrigerator.

> **TIP:**
>
> *These fruit-infused brandies make excellent gifts during the holidays and are an easy and thoughtful item to drop off to a friend on a random Tuesday. Such fun to sip on a chilly evening or add to a hot cider.*

Beer and Grapefruit Spritzers

Yes, you've read this correctly. Light and delicious beer makes its debut as a fruity, fun summertime drink. I have the sweetest of friends named Malia. She is always in my corner, cheering me on or texting me snippets of humor just when I need it most. We met in a grocery store years ago and never looked back. She introduced me to this wildly delicious beer with heavy grapefruit notes, which has become our favorite brew to drink while contemplating just how to take over the world. I came up with this drink just for her. Make it for a sweet friend who lets you be you each and every day and takes you as you are.

Prep time: 5 minutes • Yield: 2 quarts

4 (12-ounce) cans of your favorite light beer, chilled (Hefeweizen, pilsners, or light ales work beautifully. If you like a bit more of a bite, go with an IPA.)

2 cups freshly squeezed ruby red grapefruit juice, chilled

1 grapefruit, sliced with peel intact

Combine beer, grapefruit juice, and grapefruit slices in a large pitcher. Pour the beer slowly against the side of the pitcher to avoid a large amount of foam. Serve in chilled glasses.

Homemade Cold Brew with Brown Sugar Syrup

Yield: 1 quart

COLD BREW

½ cup ground coffee (for French
   press, use a slightly larger grind)

BROWN SUGAR SYRUP

1 cup brown sugar

1 cup warm water

Mix the coffee with 4 cups water in a container with a tight-sealing lid. Mix well and allow to steep in the fridge 24 hours. Remove the coffee, and pour it through a fine mesh sieve or filter. Place the cold brew in a jar. It keeps in the fridge for several days. Serve over ice with cream and brown sugar syrup.

Make the brown sugar syrup by dissolving brown sugar in warm water. This keeps in the fridge for up to 7 days.

Virgin Mary Mix

Yield: 1 quart

2–3 celery stalks

3 tablespoons cold water

3 cups low-sodium tomato
vegetable juice

1–2 tablespoons hot sauce

1 tablespoon Worcestershire
sauce

Juice and zest of 1 lemon

2 teaspoons prepared horseradish

¼ teaspoon celery seeds or salt

¼ teaspoon ground turmeric

Salt and pepper to taste

Garnish options: olives, bacon,
shrimp or crab, pepperoncini,
jalapeños, bell pepper slices,
celery stalks

Use a juicer or blend celery stalks in your blender with the cold water. Strain the mixture to get the celery juice you'll need for the mix. Depending on the celery's water content, this will yield about ½ cup. Combine with all remaining ingredients in a quart-sized jar.

This mixture is best when enjoyed within three days of preparation. Store in the refrigerator at all times. Mix with ice and vodka for an incredible Bloody Mary, or enjoy as is for a morning pick-me-up.

Cinnamon Hot Chocolate with Soft Whipped Cream

Prep time: 10 minutes • Yield: 1 quart

CINNAMON HOT CHOCOLATE

2 cups cream

2 cups whole milk

½ cup chopped dark chocolate

½ cup unsweetened cocoa powder

½ cup sugar

½ teaspoon ground cinnamon

1 pinch sea salt

1 teaspoon vanilla extract

SOFT WHIPPED CREAM

1 cup heavy cream

2 tablespoons sugar

1 teaspoon vanilla extract

1 pinch sea salt

Bring all the cinnamon hot chocolate ingredients to a simmer over medium heat. Do not boil. Reduce heat to low. The entire process should take less than 10 minutes. The hot chocolate may have a dappled look due to the fat content in the cream and chocolate. Serve with a cinnamon stick and a spoonful of soft whipped cream.

Make the soft whipped cream by whipping the cream, sugar, vanilla, and salt by hand or with a mixer until peaks have just formed but it's still quite loose.

Homemade Chai Tea Concentrate

I think many of us have enjoyed a delicious chai tea when the months get chilly. You are essentially brewing a very spicy cup of tea that will need to be mixed with milk or water to be drinkable.

Prep time: 20 minutes • Yield: roughly 1 quart

8 green cardamom pods, cracked

5 packets or 5 teaspoons loose
  leaf black tea

½ cup brown sugar

5–6 cinnamon sticks

2 star anise

1 teaspoon pumpkin pie spice

1 vanilla bean, split with seeds
  scraped out

> **TIP:**
>
> *This concentrate is an excellent addition to cake recipes that call for milk or water, as it adds a spiced, floral aroma and flavor. Simply swap out part or all of the liquid called for.*

Place all the ingredients in a medium-sized saucepan with 4 to 5 cups water. Bring to a boil, and reduce heat to low. Simmer 15 minutes. Remove from the heat, and allow to cool. Pour the concentrate through a fine mesh sieve. Discard the tea and spices. Store in a lidded quart jar in the refrigerator up to two weeks.

To serve, add ¼ cup concentrate to ½ to ¾ cups water, milk, or half-and-half, to taste. This is delicious hot or iced.

Mulled Wine

Prep time: 5 minutes • Cook time: 15 minutes • Yield: 8–10 servings

1 (750 mL) bottle Shiraz, zinfandel, or cabernet

2 cups fresh apple cider

2 cups fresh squeezed tangerine juice

4–6 green cardamom pods

2–4 cinnamon sticks

2–3 star anise

2 navel oranges, zest sliced into long strips

2 navel oranges, cut into rounds for garnish

1 Granny Smith apple, sliced into thin rounds

1 cup dried cranberries

Pour all the ingredients into a large soup pot, and heat over medium heat until it's just come to a simmer, about 15 minutes. Do not boil. Turn heat to very low to keep warm, and serve throughout the evening, or place in a slow cooker on low.

Hot Lemonade Tea

Prep time: 15 minutes • Yield: 4 8-ounce servings

4 lemons, zest cut in long strips, then juiced

½ cup honey

3 black tea bags

1 pinch Himalayan pink salt

Bring 32 ounces of water to a boil, and turn off the heat. Add lemon juice, zest, honey, tea bags, and salt, and steep for six minutes. This tea is wonderful for sore throats and stores easily in the refrigerator for about 2 days.

Strawberry Bellini

Strawberry Bellini

Prep time: 5 minutes • Yield: 4 servings

2 cups fresh strawberries

½ cup apple juice

1 tablespoon sugar

Squeeze of lemon

1 (750 mL) bottle chilled prosecco or champagne

Blitz strawberries, apple juice, sugar, and lemon in a blender or food processor until smooth, about 2 minutes. Place 2 to 3 tablespoons in a glass and top with champagne or Prosecco.

Creamy Coconut and Vodka Punch

Prep time: 5 minutes • Yield: roughly 2 quarts

1 orange, sliced

2 limes, sliced

8 to 12 ounces lemonade concentrate (depending on how sweet you'd like it), found in the freezer section of your grocery

16 ounces Coco Lopez or cream of coconut

8 ounces Heritage Distilling Mango Vodka

8 ounces Heritage Distilling Coconut Vodka

24 ounces mango or lime sparkling water

2 to 3 cups ice

In a large serving pitcher, muddle the citrus with the lemonade concentrate. Add the cream of coconut and flavored vodkas. Top with the sparkling water and ice. Stir and serve. If you are making this punch in advance, add everything except ice to the pitcher. When ready to serve, add ice.

Peachy Basil Lemonade

Prep time: 5 minutes • Yield: roughly 2 quarts

1 (12-ounce) container all-natural
frozen lemonade

2 juicy ripe peaches, sliced
½ cup torn basil leaves

36 ounces seltzer water

Use the lemonade concentrate container, which is 12 ounces, to measure all the liquid. Muddle the peaches, basil, and lemonade concentrate. Slowly stir in the seltzer water, and top with more sliced peaches and basil to serve!

Closing Thoughts

Your home and what you have in it are perfect.

You are gifted and special. Your home and what you have in it are perfect. I know it. Don't wait to be generous with your time or life or love. Do it now. You do have community. At any time, choose to open your heart and your home and build relationships. It's not always easy. In fact, it's tough sometimes. Our hearts were designed for fellowship and laughter and delicious food.

This life we live is beautiful, but it's easy to get caught up in the pressures of family, work, and everyday living. We live in a world today that values the "more is more" model—faster, quicker, better than the last. It's hard to keep up. I don't want to live my life in a pressure cooker. I don't want my children to recall the way they grew up as too hurried and loaded to the brim with endless activities. Even things that are good and healthy can become too much—too many sports after school, too many music lessons, too many playdate obligations that leave us scrambling from task to task. Do you fall into bed at night sometimes in tears because you feel like you can't keep up? When your life is filled with tasks, obligations, and places to be, you turn inward, searching for the fortitude to simply get through. Sharing—community—is the antidote to this way of living. Sharing encourages you, with a gentle hand, to look outward, to search for harmony in a place you can't reach alone.

Growing up, my siblings and I participated in many activities, but we didn't feel crushed by them. We spent Sundays in church and picnicking. Not fancy picnics with pretty gingham and wicker baskets, just a loaded cooler and a blanket, all of us headed in the car to Mount Rainier. We'd crawl down by the streams from a side road in the park and eat egg salad sandwiches and taco chips washed down with water from a thermos, bottles of Dr. Pepper, or Kool-Aid. Big, ultra-thin chocolate chip cookies with crisp edges always served quite nicely as dessert. We played long and hard outside during the summers, and when in school, I don't remember a gaggle of homework and practices after school

The way I want to entertain and invite people into my home is with heart and soul, not perfection.

daily. There seemed to be this way of life we had growing up, and it's a way of living I want now for my own family—a way of living that pays tribute to values that can't be measured by dollars or status. It's a way of living that appreciates togetherness. When life feels a little slippery these days, I often think of my childhood, which was not perfect but was somehow perfectly rough around the edges. It guides me back to a good place.

Though I strenuously advocate for the practice of sharing, I've absolutely felt the pressures of entertaining. Sometimes it can feel counterproductive to have people over. There's cleaning for hours, cooking all the food, trying to just be okay or even to impress when your heart just isn't buying in. I've been there. But recently, I had the opportunity to spend a week in the home of a woman who told me she wants people to feel like they've been given a hug when they come through her front doors. And hugged I felt. She was succeeding admirably. What a tidy but powerful sentiment, to make your guests feel like they've been given a hug. It was relaxing to be far out in the country, in Leiper's Fork, Tennessee, where lightning bugs dance on the lawn at dusk and the air smells sweet, like freshly cut hay. There were beautiful cranes and wild turkeys roaming the fields in and among the cattle. There were drooping trees and this golden sunlight that was life-giving. Even though at home I may not have all this sensory splendor to offer my guests, I still believe I have the ability to make visitors feel hugged when they walk through my door. I can definitely do that.

The way I want to entertain and invite people into my home is with heart and soul, not perfection. And you don't always have to have people over to share. I want to drop food off and give a big ol' hug and say, "God hasn't forgotten you. You are going to be okay." Or maybe something simple like, "Hey, I love you, and you don't have to cook tonight. Enjoy the meal!" Then I'd just hightail it out of there and be on my way. I love giving people food. I truly do—it's what I know. Giving people dinner makes me feel loved and helps me to show love. I never worry about matching dishes coordinated with the color scheme of the linens; most of the time, it's paper plates and foil tins and food that is cooked with heart, soul, and great care in mind, not visual perfection.

Taste is far more fulfilling than culinary aesthetics here! I'll take a messy, rustic pie slice over a meticulously decorated slice of cake any day of the week.

When Milo was in the NICU after birth, my sweet friend met me in the hospital parking lot and filled my car with groceries, quick meals, and clothes for the baby. I stood there dumbfounded. Was this real life? At that point, everything seemed to be falling down around Mike and me, but this was one of the sweetest blessings I'd ever been given. To feed people truly is the best way to love them. It's never just food being given; it's time and energy, and it's a statement of inclusiveness. It says *Hey, it's time we spent time together again*. Community is powerful and healing.

Just recently, there was a week when Mike and I had serious work to do. I mean plenty of work, the kind of work where if you consider the to-do list for more than a second, tears start to well up! During this same week, my parents and my sister's family were taking a road trip to Reno, Nevada, to visit my grandfather. We

CLOSING THOUGHTS

were invited, but I told them we couldn't possibly go, there was too much to do; we couldn't spare the time. Then my son, who'd caught wind of the trip somehow, packed his backpack and put his swim trunks on and stood by the front door, crying, "C'mon, Mom! Please! We need to be with our family." There was much hemming and hawing, but ultimately, we threw clothes in bags, grabbed snacks from the pantry, and shoved off to catch our family on the road. You see, sometimes work can wait. Deadlines can wait. Projects can wait. Computers can be packed up, and work-related emails can be sent from the road. (Technology is crazy these days!) Not always, but *sometimes* business can wait…just a bit.

But my darling eight-year-old boy won't wait. He won't be on the doorstep forever, begging his mama to take him to the park with his cousins. He won't always want the long snuggles his parents are happy to provide or to hunt for tree frogs in the front yard with his dad. He keeps growing, changing, and becoming a man. Right now, he's into family-road-trip continental breakfasts at economy hotels, wrestling on the floor with his little brother, and riding scooters with the kids down the block. He wants to run and play with his buds all day, then fall into bed at night, sticky with sweat. These things can't wait. These activities are *his* way of sharing in the beauty of living. I am trying to show my babies that to share is to live life to its fullest. It's up to me to cultivate this sense of community inside them, to encourage them toward an appreciation of time spent with Grandma and Papa while they still grace the earth. That's why we ended up on our little road trip to Reno with the family. I wouldn't trade playing nickel slots in the casino with my eighty-five-year-old grandmother whose jaw drops hilariously when I bet anything more than twenty-five cents! I would not trade walkie-talkie caravans through Lassen National Forest or ice cream cones in ninety-degree heat at Burney Falls in California for any amount of met deadlines or checked-off to-do lists.

Let's live. Let's truly live and find balance in our lives. Let's practice "the art of no." Let's eat melons wrapped in prosciutto on our porch with friends and talk about life and laugh, with dishes in the sink and clothes needing washing and work needing done. Let's find a way to invite friendship in again when too much time has passed between hangouts. Let's just share.

People like to tell me all the fanciest foods they've been eating, and they often ask what fine dining establishments I've visited as of late. I never really have an answer because "the family meal," as it's known in the restaurant world, is what I'm after. Peasant food. I want the tough cuts braised all day, I want the potatoes mashed with the skins on, and I want all the time with people I love. I need to breathe in this life today, in the moment, because it's good for the soul. I want to come after life with a heart of gratitude and praise the Lord for the breath in my lungs and all His provision, even when it comes after much hardship. I want the joy in my life to always be held in the journey and the loving and the doing well by people. Because this life is truly a gift, and it's meant to be shared.

Let's truly live and find balance in our lives. Let's find a way to invite friendship in again when too much time has passed between hangouts. Let's just share.

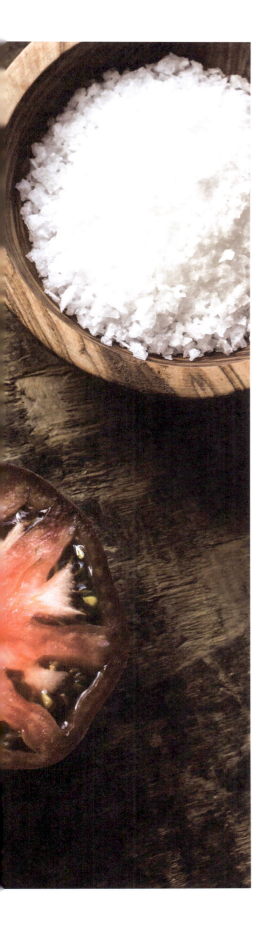

Index

Note: Page numbers in *italic* refer to photographs.

A

Aioli and Roasted Artichokes, 110

Aioli, Sun-Dried Tomato, 92, *92*

Albondigas (Enchilada Meatballs), 53, *54*

apples

    Apple Butter Crumb Cake, *178*, 179

    Apple Cinnamon Monkey Bread, *134*, 135

    Apple Cranberry Shortbread Crumble, 172, *173*

    Noah's Apple Cake, 175

Apricot and Chocolate Rolls, 151

Artichokes and Aioli, Roasted, 110

asparagus

    Garlicky Asparagus, 114, *114*

    Oven-Roasted Lemon-Pepper Asparagus, 79

INDEX 221

B

Bacon, Tomato, and Mushroom Campanelle, 20, *21*

Banana Cream Pudding, Caramelized, 180, *181*

Barbecue Chicken Legs, *90*, 91

Bars, Cherry Pie, 136, *137*

basil

Melon with Basil and Prosciutto, 122, *123*

Peachy Basil Lemonade, *212*, 213

Spinach and Basil Pesto, 10, *82*, 84

Strawberry Basil Relish, 48, *49*

beans

See also green beans

Cassoulet with Chicken Thighs and Sausages, 9–10, *11*

Refried Beans, 55

Sheet Pan Chicken Nachos, 76, 77

Tuscan Veggie and Chickpea Stew, 24, *25*

Béchamel, Garlic and Parmesan, 39

beef

Beer-Braised Chuck Roast, 15, *16*, 17

Charcuterie and Cheese, *124*, 125

Enchilada Meatballs (Albondigas), 53, *54*

Ground Beef Stroganoff, *26*, 27

Last Meatball Recipe You'll Ever Need, The, *82*, 83

Ranch Smash Burgers, 85, *86*

Steak "Dianna," 28, *29*

Beer and Grapefruit Spritzers, *196*, 197

Beer-Braised Chuck Roast, 15, *16*, 17

Bellini, Strawberry, *208*, 209

beverages, 183–213

Biscuits, Flaky Cream, *138*, 139

Blueberry Pound Cake, Wild Dried, 167

Brandy, Pear, 195

Bread Crumb Topping, Buttered, with Classic Baked Shells and Cheese, 79

Bread Crumbs, Pan-Fried Butter and Herb, 10, *11*

Bread Crumbs, with Garlic and Anchovy Spaghetti, 80

breads and bread dishes

See also sandwiches; toast

Apple Cinnamon Monkey Bread, *134*, 135

Apricot and Chocolate Rolls, 151

Buttery Dinner Rolls, 89

Cheesy Breadsticks, 67

Cheesy Scallion Soda Bread, 24, *25*

Chocolate Chip Pumpkin Bread, 152, *153*

Flaky Cream Biscuits, *138*, 139

Focaccia, 93

Garlic Knots, 64, *65*

Peach and Heirloom Tomato Panzanella, 122

Brie and Heirloom Tomato Toast, 121

broccoli

Parmesan Skillet Broccoli, 27

Sesame Broccoli, 73

Brussels Sprouts, Apple Cider, 81

Burgers, Ranch Smash, 85, *86*

222 INDEX

C

Caesar Dressing, 117

cakes

    Apple Butter Crumb Cake, *178, 179*

    Apple Cinnamon Monkey Bread, *134, 135*

    Cream Coconut Cake, 156, *157*

    Lime Tres Leches Cake, *140, 141*

    Molten Chocolate and Caramel Cakes, 176, *177*

    Noah's Apple Cake, 175

    Olive Oil and Espresso Dark Chocolate
        Cake with Cream Cheese Buttercream
        and Caramel, *170*, 171

    One-Pan Lava Cake, *174*, 175

    Pineapple Cloud Cake, *154*, 155

    Pumpkin Tiramisu, *142, 143*

    Tender Gingerbread Cake, 144, *145*

    Wild Dried Blueberry Pound Cake, 167

Caramel and Cream Cheese Buttercream, Salted, *170*, 171

Caramel and Molten Chocolate Cakes, 176, *177*

Caramel, Citrus, with Vanilla Panna Cotta, *146*, 147

Caramelized Banana Cream Pudding, 180, *181*

Carrots and Parsnips, Glazed, 15, *16*, 17

Casserole, Lydia's (Creamy Celery, Leek, Potato, and Kielbasa Sausage Bake), 41–44, *42*

Cassoulet with Chicken Thighs and Sausages, 9–10, *11*

Cauliflower Mashed Potatoes, *29*, 30

Celery and Blue Cheese Salad, Crunchy, 118, *119*

Chai Tea Concentrate, Homemade, 203

Charcuterie and Cheese, *124*, 125

cheese

    Brie and Heirloom Tomato Toast, 121

    Charcuterie and Cheese, *124*, 125

    Cheddar and Dill Baked Potato Soup, *18*, 19

    Cheesy Breadsticks, 67

    Cheesy Scallion Soda Bread, 24, *25*

    Classic Baked Shells and Cheese, 79

    Focaccia MLTs (Mozzarella, Lettuce, and Tomato), 93–95, *94*

    Fresh Fig and Soft Cheese Toast, *126*, 127, *129*

    Pan-Fried Cheese Sandwiches, 97

cherries

    Cherry Pie Bars, 136, *137*

    Short-Crust Sour Cherry Cobbler, 148, *149*

chicken. *See* poultry

Chili-Lime Pineapple Spears, 78, *78*

Chimichurri Chicken Meatballs, 45–47, *46*

chocolate

    Apricot and Chocolate Rolls, 151

    Basic Not-Basic Chocolate Cream Pie, *160*, 161

    Chocolate Almond Coconut Granola Sundae, 166

    Chocolate Chip Pumpkin Bread, 152, *153*

    Chocolate Peanut Butter Tart, *164*, 165

    Chocolate Sauce for Dipping, 168, *169*

    Churros con Chocolate, 168, *169*

    Magic Shell and Pistachio Sundaes, 162, *163*

    Molten Chocolate and Caramel Cakes, 176, *177*

    Olive Oil and Espresso Dark Chocolate
        Cake with Cream Cheese Buttercream
        and Caramel, *170*, 171

One-Pan Lava Cake, *174*, 175

Pumpkin Tiramisu, *142*, 143

Chow Mein Noodles with Sweet 'n' Sour Chicken, *56*, 57–58

Churros con Chocolate, 168, *169*

Cinnamon Cream Glaze, *178*, 179

Cinnamon Hot Chocolate with Soft Whipped Cream, 202

Cinnamon-Sugar Dredge, 168, *169*

Citronette, 74

Cobbler, Short-Crust Sour Cherry, 148, *149*

Coconut and Vodka Punch, Creamy, 210, *211*

Coconut Cake, Cream, 156, *157*

coffee

Homemade Cold Brew with Brown Sugar Syrup, 198, *199*

Olive Oil and Espresso Dark Chocolate Cake with Cream Cheese Buttercream and Caramel, *170*, 171

Pumpkin Tiramisu, *142*, 143

Coleslaw, Creamy Traditional, 92, *92*

condiments. *See* sauces and toppings

Corn and Zucchini Fritters, 91, *92*

Couscous, Herb and Parmesan Israeli, 48, *49*

Cranberry Apple Shortbread Crumble, 172, *173*

Cream Cheese Buttercream and Caramel, *170*, 171

Cream Cheese Whipped Cream, 141

Crème de Cassis, *188*, 189–190, *191*

Croutons, Olive Oil, 117

Crumb Cake, Apple Butter, *178*, 179

Crumble, Apple Cranberry Shortbread, 172, *173*

cucumbers

Frisée Salad, 67

Quick Pickled Cucumbers, 109

Smashed Cucumber and Pesto Salad, 10

D

desserts, 131–181

Dinner Rolls, Buttery, 89

drinks, 183–213

E

Eggplant Parmesan, 66

Eggs, Soft-Boiled, and Green Beans with Hazelnut and Lemon Vinaigrette Toast, *126*, 128

Enchilada Meatballs (Albondigas), 53, *54*

F

Fig and Soft Cheese Toast, Fresh, *126*, 127, 129

fish

Baked Salmon with Strawberry Basil Relish, 48, *49*

Fiery, Sweet Asian Salmon with Rice Noodles and Quick Pickled Cucumbers, 107–109, *108*

Pan-Seared Dill and Caper Halibut, *112*, 113, *114*

Focaccia MLTs (Mozzarella, Lettuce, and Tomato), 93–95, *94*

Fries, Sweet Potato, *94*, *95*

Frisée Salad, 67

Fritters, Zucchini and Fresh Corn, 91, *92*

G

Garlic and Lemon Cacio e Pepe, 110, *111*

Garlic and Parmesan Béchamel, 39

Garlic Knots, 64, *65*

Garlic Toast, 6, 7

Garlicky Asparagus, 114, *114*

Garlicky Chanterelles, *62*, 63

Garlicky Green Beans, 87

Ginger Peanut Noodles, 106

Gingerbread Cake, Tender, 144, *145*

Glaze, Cinnamon Cream, *178*, 179

Granola Chocolate Almond Sundae, 166

Grapefruit and Beer Spritzers, *196*, 197

green beans

Chimichurri Chicken Meatballs with
Herbed Greek Yogurt, Red Quinoa,
and Green Beans, 45–47, *46*

Garlicky Green Beans, 87

Soft-Boiled Eggs and Green Beans with Hazelnut
and Lemon Vinaigrette Toast, *126*, 128

greens

See also salads

Sausage and Leek Puff Pastry Pie, 22

Sautéed Swiss Chard, 14

Guacamole, Fresh, 76, 77

H

Halibut, Pan-Seared Dill and Caper, *112*, 113,
114

Hamburgers, Ranch Smash, 85, *86*

Hazelnut and Lemon Vinaigrette, 128

Herb and Pan-Fried Butter Bread Crumbs, 10,
11

Herb and Parmesan Israeli Couscous, 48, *49*

Herbed Greek Yogurt, 45, *46*

Honey Mustard, Lemony, 44

Hot Chocolate with Soft Whipped Cream,
Cinnamon, 202

I

Irish Cream Mason Jars to Go, *192*, 193

Israeli Couscous, Herb and Parmesan, 48, *49*

K

Kabobs, Grilled Lamb, 74, *75*

Knots, Garlic, 64, *65*

INDEX 225

L

lamb
Grilled Lamb Kabobs, 74, *75*
Zesty Buffalo-Style Rack of Lamb, 118, *119*
Lasagna, Creamy Sausage and Mushroom, *38*, 39–40
leeks
Lydia's Casserole (Creamy Celery, Leek, Potato, and Kielbasa Sausage Bake), 41–44, *42*
Sausage and Leek Puff Pastry Pie, *22*
Lemon and Hazelnut Vinaigrette, 128
Lemonade, Peachy Basil, *212*, 213
Lemonade Tea, Hot, 206, *207*
Lemony Honey Mustard, 44
Lime-Chili Pineapple Spears, 78, *78*
Lime Tart, Creamy, *158*, 159
Lime Tres Leches Cake, *140*, 141
Limoncello, Homemade, *186*, 187
Lobster Dinner Splurge, 115, *116*
Lydia's Casserole (Creamy Celery, Leek, Potato, and Kielbasa Sausage Bake), 41–44, *42*

M

Mâché Caesar Salad, 117
Magic Shell and Pistachio Sundaes, 162, *163*
Marshmallow Treats, Double Peanut, 150
meatballs
Chimichurri Chicken Meatballs, 45–47, *46*

Enchilada Meatballs (Albondigas), 53, *54*
Last Meatball Recipe You'll Ever Need, The, *82*, 83
Melon with Basil and Prosciutto, 122, *123*
Milk Drench, 141
MLTs (Mozzarella, Lettuce, and Tomato), Focaccia, 93–95, *94*
Monkey Bread, Apple Cinnamon, *134*, 135
Mulled Wine, *204*, 205
mushrooms
Bacon, Tomato, and Mushroom Campanelle, 20, *21*
Butter Lettuce and Mushroom Salad, 52
Creamy Sausage and Mushroom Lasagna, *38*, 39–40
Garlicky Chanterelles, 62, *63*
Ground Beef Stroganoff, 26, *27*
Mustard, Lemony Honey, 44

N

Nachos, Sheet Pan Chicken, 76, 77
Noah's Apple Cake, 175
noodles. *See* pasta

O

Olive Oil and Espresso Dark Chocolate Cake with Cream Cheese Buttercream and Caramel, *170*, 171
Olive Oil Croutons, 117

P

Pan Sauce, 28

Pancetta Polenta, 13–14

Panna Cotta with Citrus Caramel, Vanilla, *146*, 147

Panzanella, Peach and Heirloom Tomato, 122

Parsnips and Carrots, Glazed, 15, *16*, 17

pasta

Bacon, Tomato, and Mushroom Campanelle, 20, *21*

Boneless Braised Pork Spareribs with Garlicky Chanterelles and Spaetzle, *62*, 63

Classic Baked Shells and Cheese, 79

Creamy Sausage and Mushroom Lasagna, *38*, 39–40

Creamy Tomato Baked Ziti, 6, 7

Crispy Sweet Chili and Sesame Shrimp with Ginger Peanut Noodles, *104*, 105–106

Fiery, Sweet Asian Salmon with Rice Noodles and Quick Pickled Cucumbers, 107–109, *108*

Garlic and Anchovy Spaghetti with Bread Crumbs, 80

Garlic and Lemon Cacio e Pepe, 110, *111*

Ground Beef Stroganoff, *26*, 27

Last Meatball Recipe You'll Ever Need, The, Creamy Orzo, and Spinach and Basil Pesto, 82, 83–84

Parmesan Ditalini and Peas, 88

Pesto and Mozzarella Pasta, 59, *61*

Shrimp and Chive Penne, 64, *65*

Spicy, Fresh Heirloom Tomato Bucatini with Brie, *120*, 121

Sweet 'n' Sour Chicken with Cheap Chow Mein, 56, *57–58*

peaches

Peach and Heirloom Tomato Panzanella, 122

Peachy Basil Lemonade, *212*, 213

Peanut Marshmallow Treats, Double, 150

Pear Brandy, 195

Peas and Ditalini, Parmesan, 88

pesto

Pesto and Mozzarella Pasta, 59, *61*

Red Pesto Dressing, 23

Spinach and Basil Pesto, 10, 82, 84

Pickled Cucumbers, Quick, 109

Pie, Basic Not-Basic Chocolate Cream, *160*, 161

piment d'Espelette, 9

pineapple

Chili-Lime Pineapple Spears, 78, *78*

Pineapple Cloud Cake, *154*, 155

Pistachio and Magic Shell Sundaes, 162, *163*

Pistachio-Crusted Chicken Cutlets, 31, *32*, *33*

Polenta, Pancetta, 13–14

pork

Bacon, Tomato, and Mushroom Campanelle, 20, *21*

Boneless Braised Pork Spareribs, *62*, 63

Melon with Basil and Prosciutto, 122, *123*

Pancetta Polenta, 13–14

Sticky, Spicy Oven-Baked Baby Back Ribs, *72*, 73

potatoes

Cauliflower Mashed Potatoes, *29*, 30

Cheddar and Dill Baked Potato Soup, *18*, 19

Dauphinoise Potatoes, 115

Lydia's Casserole (Creamy Celery, Leek, Potato, and Kielbasa Sausage Bake), 41–44, *42*

Potato Wedges, 87

Sour Cream Smashed Potatoes, *16, 17,* 17

poultry

Barbecue Chicken Legs, *90,* 91

Buttermilk Grilled Chicken, 88

Cassoulet with Chicken Thighs and Sausages, 9–10, *11*

Chicken Caesar Toast, *126,* 128

Chimichurri Chicken Meatballs, 45–47, *46*

Coq au Vin with Pancetta Polenta, 13–14

Enchilada Meatballs (Albondigas), 53, *54*

Italian Rocket and Chicken Salad, 60, *61*

Pistachio-Crusted Chicken Cutlets, 31, *32, 33*

Sheet Pan Chicken Nachos, 76, 77

Sweet 'n' Sour Chicken, *56,* 57

Pound Cake, Wild Dried Blueberry, 167

Prosciutto and Basil with Melon, 122, *123*

Pudding, Caramelized Banana Cream, 180, *181*

Puff Pastry Pie, Sausage and Leek, *22*

pumpkin

Chocolate Chip Pumpkin Bread, 152, *153*

Creamy Tomato and Pumpkin Soup, *96,* 97

Pumpkin Tiramisu, *142, 143*

Punch, Creamy Coconut and Vodka, 210, *211*

Punch, Mom's Wine, 194

Q

quinoa

Chimichurri Chicken Meatballs with Herbed Greek Yogurt, Red Quinoa, and Green Beans, 45–47, *46*

Red Quinoa and Tomato Grain Salad, *74, 75*

R

Ranch Dressing, 85, *86*

Ratatouille, Stovetop, *29,* 30

Refried Beans, 55

Relish, Strawberry Basil, 48, *49*

ribs. *See* pork

rice

Black Pepper and Parmesan Risotto, 113, *114*

Spanish Rice, *54, 55*

rolls

Apricot and Chocolate Rolls, 151

Buttery Dinner Rolls, 89

roux, 39

Rustic Joyful Food, about, xv, xvii–xix

S

salads

Boston Buttermilk Salad, 40

Butter Lettuce and Mushroom Salad, 52

Crunchy Celery and Blue Cheese Salad, 118, *119*

Frisée Salad, 67

Greens and Red Pesto Dressing, 23

Heirloom Tomato and Ricotta Salad, *32, 33, 33*

Italian Rocket and Chicken Salad, 60, *61*

Mâché Caesar Salad, 117

Mixed Greens and Lemony Honey Mustard, 44

Olive Oil Croutons for, 117

Red Quinoa and Tomato Grain Salad, 74, *75*

Salami Chopped Salad, 6, 8

Smashed Cucumber and Pesto Salad, 10

Spinach and Parmesan Salad, 20, *21*

Salami Chopped Salad, 6, 8

salmon

Baked Salmon with Strawberry Basil Relish, 48, *49*

Fiery, Sweet Asian Salmon with Rice Noodles and Quick Pickled Cucumbers, 107–109, *108*

sandwiches and burgers

Focaccia MLTs (Mozzarella, Lettuce, and Tomato), 93–95, *94*

Pan-Fried Cheese Sandwiches, 97

Ranch Smash Burgers, 85, *86*

sauces and toppings

See also pesto

Buttered Bread Crumb Topping, 79

Chocolate Sauce for Dipping, 168, *169*

Cinnamon Cream Glaze, *178, 179*

Cream Cheese Buttercream and Caramel, *170, 171*

Cream Cheese Whipped Cream, 141

Enchilada Sauce, 53

Fresh Guacamole, 76, *77*

Garlic and Parmesan Béchamel, 39

Hazelnut and Lemon Vinaigrette, 128

Herbed Greek Yogurt, 45, *46*

Pan-Fried Butter and Herb Bread Crumbs, 10, *11*

Pan Sauce, 28

Ranch Dressing, 85, *86*

Roasted Artichokes and Aioli, 110

Soft Whipped Cream, 159, 202

Strawberry Basil Relish, 48, *49*

Sun-Dried Tomato Aioli, 92, *92*

Sweet 'n' Sour Sauce, *56, 57*

sausage

Cassoulet with Chicken Thighs and Sausages, 9–10, *11*

Creamy Sausage and Mushroom Lasagna, *38, 39–40*

Last Meatball Recipe You'll Ever Need, The, *82, 83*

Lydia's Casserole (Creamy Celery, Leek, Potato, and Kielbasa Sausage Bake), 41–44, *42*

Salami Chopped Salad, 6, 8

Sausage and Leek Puff Pastry Pie, 22

seafood and fish

Baked Salmon with Strawberry Basil Relish, 48, *49*

Crispy Sweet Chili and Sesame Shrimp with Ginger Peanut Noodles, *104, 105–106*

Fiery, Sweet Asian Salmon with Rice Noodles and Quick Pickled Cucumbers, 107–109, *108*

Lobster Dinner Splurge, 115, *116*

Pan-Seared Dill and Caper Halibut, *112, 113, 114*

Quick Creole Shrimp Étouffée, *50,* 51

Shrimp and Chive Penne, 64, *65*

Shortbread Crumble, Apple Cranberry, 172, *173*

shrimp. *See* seafood and fish

Soda Bread, Cheesy Scallion, 24, *25*

soups and stews

Cassoulet with Chicken Thighs
and Sausages, 9–10, *11*

Cheddar and Dill Baked Potato Soup, *18,* 19

Creamy Tomato and Pumpkin Soup, *96, 97*

Tuscan Veggie and Chickpea Stew, 24, *25*

Sour Cream Dressing, 85, *86*

Spanish Rice, *54, 55*

spinach

Pesto and Mozzarella Pasta, 59, *61*

Spinach and Basil Pesto, 10, *82, 84*

Spinach and Parmesan Salad, 20, *21*

Spritzers, Beer and Grapefruit, *196,* 197

squash

See also pumpkin

Stovetop Ratatouille, 29, 30

Zucchini and Fresh Corn Fritters, 91, *92*

strawberries

Strawberry Basil Relish, 48, *49*

Strawberry Bellini, *208,* 209

Sun-Dried Tomato Aioli, 92, *92*

sundaes

Chocolate Almond Coconut Granola Sundae, 166

Magic Shell and Pistachio Sundaes, 162, *163*

Sweet 'n' Sour Chicken with Cheap Chow Mein,
56, 57–58

Sweet Potato Fries, *94,* 95

sweets, 131–181

Swiss Chard, Sautéed, 14

T

tarts

Chocolate Peanut Butter Tart, *164,* 165

Creamy Lime Tart, *158, 159*

tea

Homemade Chai Tea Concentrate, 203

Hot Lemonade Tea, 206, *207*

Tiramisu, Pumpkin, *142,* 143

toast

Brie and Heirloom Tomato Toast, 121

Chicken Caesar Toast, *126, 128*

Fresh Fig and Soft Cheese Toast, *126, 127, 129*

Garlic Toast, 6, 7

Soft-Boiled Eggs and Green Beans with Hazelnut
and Lemon Vinaigrette Toast, *126,* 123

tomatoes

Bacon, Tomato, and Mushroom Camparelle, 20, *21*

Brie and Heirloom Tomato Toast, 121

Creamy Tomato and Pumpkin Soup, 96, 97

Creamy Tomato Baked Ziti with Garlic Toast, 6, 7

Eggplant Parmesan, 66

Focaccia MLTs (Mozzarella, Lettuce,
and Tomato), 93–95, *94*

Heirloom Tomato and Ricotta Salad, *32*, 33, *33*
Peach and Heirloom Tomato Panzanella, 122
Red Quinoa and Tomato Grain Salad, 74, *75*
Spicy, Fresh Heirloom Tomato Bucatini, *120*, 121
Sun-Dried Tomato Aioli, *92*, 92

toppings. *See* sauces and toppings

V

Vanilla Panna Cotta with Citrus Caramel, *146*, 147
Vinaigrette, Hazelnut and Lemon, 128
Virgin Mary Mix, *200*, 201

W

Whipped Cream, Cream Cheese, 141
Whipped Cream, Soft, 159, 202
Wine, Mulled, *204*, 205
Wine Punch, Mom's, 194

Y

Yogurt, Herbed Greek, 45, *46*

Z

zucchini
Stovetop Ratatouille, *29*, 30
Zucchini and Fresh Corn Fritters, 91, *92*

About the Author

Danielle Kartes

Danielle Kartes is an author and recipe developer living near Seattle, Washington, with her photographer husband, Michael, and their two sweet boys, Noah and Milo. Together, the Karteses run their boutique food and lifestyle company, Rustic Joyful Food. Rustic Joyful Food promotes loving your life right where you are, no matter where you are, and creating beautiful, delicious, fuss-free food with whatever you have available to you. Danielle appears regularly on national television and speaks publicly at events around the country.